CATASTROPHE INSURANCE:
Consumer Demand, Markets and Regulation

Topics in Regulatory Economics and Policy Series

Michael A. Crew, Editor
Center for Research in Regulated Industries
Graduate School of Management, Rutgers University
Newark, New Jersey, U.S.A.

Previously published books in the series:

Zaccour, G.:
Deregulation of Electric Utilities
Young, W.:
Atomic Energy Costing
Crew, M.:
Regulation Under Increasing Competition
Crew, M.A. and Kleindorfer, P. R.:
Emerging Competition in Postal and Delivery Services
Cherry, B.A.:
The Crisis in Telecommunications Carrier Liability: Historical Regulatory Flaws and Recommended Reform
Loomis, D.G. and Taylor, L. D.:
The Future of the Telecommunications Industry: Forecasting and Demand Analysis
Alleman, J. and Noam, E.:
The New Investment Theory of Real Options and its Implications for Telecommunications Economics
Crew, M. and Kleindorfer, P. R:
Current Directions in Postal Reform
Faruqui, A. and Eakin, K.
Pricing in Competitive Electricity Markets
Lehman, D. E. and Weisman, D. L.
The Telecommunications Act of 1996: The "Costs" of Managed Competition
Crew, Michael A.
Expanding Competition in Regulated Industries
Crew, M. A. and Kleindorfer, P. R.:
Future Directions in Postal Reform
Loomis, D.G. and Taylor, L.D.
Forecasting the Internet: Understanding the Explosive Growth of Data
Crew, M. A. and Schuh, J. C.
Markets, Pricing, and Deregulation of Utilities
Crew, M.A. and Kleindorfer, P.R.
Postal and Delivery Services: Pricing, Productivity, Regulation and Strategy
Faruqui, A. and Eakin, K.
Electricity Pricing in Transition
Lehr, W. H. and Pupillo, L. M.
Cyber Policy and Economics in an Internet Age
Crew, M. A. and Kleindorfer, P. R.
Postal and Delivery Services: Delivering on Competition

CATASTROPHE INSURANCE: Consumer Demand, Markets and Regulation

by

Martin F. Grace
Georgia State University
Atlanta, Georgia

Robert W. Klein
Georgia State University
Atlanta, Georgia

Paul R. Kleindorfer
University of Pennsylvania
Philadelphia, Pennsylvania

Michael R. Murray
Insurance Services Office, Inc.
Jersey City, New Jersey

Kluwer Academic Publishers
Boston/Dordecht/London

Distributors for North, Central and South America:
Kluwer Academic Publishers
101 Philip Drive
Assinippi Park
Norwell, Massachusetts 02061 USA
Telephone (781) 871-6600
Fax (781) 871-6528
E-Mail <kluwer@wkap.com>

Distributors for all other countries:
Kluwer Academic Publishers Group
Post Office Box 322
3300 AH Dordrecht, THE NETHERLANDS
Telephone 31 78 6576 000
Fax 31 78 6576 474
E-Mail <orderdept@wkap.nl>

Electronic Services <http://www.wkap.nl>

Library of Congress Cataloging-in-Publication

Title: Catastrophe Insurance: Consumer Demand, Markets and Regulation
Author: Martin F. Grace, Robert W. Klein, Paul R. Kleindorfer, and Michael R. Murray
ISBN: 1-4020-7469-7

Printed on acid-free paper.

Printed in United Kingdom by Biddles/IBT Global

CONTENTS

PREFACE AND ACKNOWLEDGEMENTS

This book is the result of a project begun at the Wharton Risk Management and Decision Processes Center in 1996 on Managing Catastrophic Risks. The project in its early days was concerned with the role of insurance and capital markets in managing catastrophic risks arising from natural hazards. Given recent events, the project has expanded its focus to deal with terrorism and other extreme events, under the project name "Managing and Financing Extreme Events". The project has profited immensely from the contributions of a number of academic and industry affiliations, most important among which have been the on-going cooperation between the Wharton Risk Center, the Wharton Financial Institutions Center, the Center for Risk Management and Insurance Research of Georgia State University and the Insurance Services Office, Inc. (ISO). Our efforts have also been complemented by input from sponsoring member institutions and research partners drawn from selected modeling and consulting firms, including AIR Worldwide Corporation, EQECAT, and Risk Management Solutions.

This has been an ambitious undertaking, and the present volume represents only one of several research initiatives in the overall project. To provide some sense of the scope of the project, we note here the five major activities that have been undertaken under the auspices of this project:

1. Mitigation of hazards via building and other retrofits: This part of the project has been concerned with assessing the effects of mitigation on expected losses, and on insurer solvency and profitability. The project has also considered the implications of such mitigation for insurance industry practices and for homeowner decisions to invest in mitigation measures.

2. Insurance regulation and industry analysis: This research entailed a large-scale empirical analysis of the supply and demand determinants of market offerings of catastrophe insurance products, and the effects of regulation on solvency and pricing of such catastrophe insurance products. The present monograph reflects the major findings of this set of activities.

3. Securitization of insurance risk: The possibility of securitizing catastrophe risks has been a centerpiece since the successful Act of God Bonds first offered by USAA. Such securities act as "options" to insurance companies. These options trigger payoffs to insurers precisely when they need them most, namely when catastrophes occur.

The project has studied the design and pricing of such securities and the determinants of their market acceptance.

4. Measuring the capacity of insurance and reinsurance markets to respond to catastrophic losses: The reason for such strong interest in catastrophic risks in the first place has been the danger these risks pose to insurers that insolvency could result from large events, such as Hurricane Andrew in 1992 or the Northridge Earthquake of 1994. The project has developed a number of conceptual and computational tools for assessing the capacity of the insurance and reinsurance industry to respond to such events.

5. Interdependent security risk: The project has recently expanded its scope to confront issues of insurability and risk management for security risks, especially those involving multiple parties whose actions may give rise to interdependencies in the mitigation or financing of such risks. The project has also been concerned with the insurance issues that arise from the ambiguity and strategic nature of the risks from terrorism and the appropriate roles for the government and private sector in managing and financing such risks.

Several important publications have resulted from the Wharton Project to date. These include the book, edited by Howard Kunreuther and Richard Roth, Sr. *Paying the Price: The Status and Role of Insurance Against Natural Disasters in the United States*, published in 1998; and the book, edited by Howard Kunreuther, Patricia Grossi and Chandu Patel, *New Approaches to the Management of Natural Hazards*, which will be published in 2003, and which is a companion volume to the present volume. The Kunreuther, Grossi and Patel volume provides an extensive overview of the theory and practice of risk assessment, catastrophe modeling and risk quantification for insurance and reinsurance purposes for natural hazards and other extreme events. The present volume provides an analysis of the institutions governing natural hazard insurance, together with a theoretical and empirical examination of the supply and demand for such insurance. Project work on securitization and capacity is reviewed in Cummins, Doherty and Lo (2002), and Cummins, Lalonde and Phillips (2002, 2003).

This monograph presents the results of the first significant attempt to examine empirically the nature of the demand for insurance against natural disasters at a detailed, microeconomic level within a regulated market. Our examination has been made possible with the unprecedented assembly of an extensive, detailed database on residential insurance transactions affected by catastrophe risk. ISO provided these data to the authors on a confidential basis, and they provided considerable assistance in interpreting the data and in assisting us in understanding and computing model loss costs for Florida and New York policies covered by the data. The insurers included in this database granted explicit permission for the authors to use these data on a confidential basis. We want to express to ISO and their respondents who contributed their data to this study our deep appreciation for their cooperation, without which this study could not have been accomplished.

Kiwan Lee was a postdoctoral fellow in the Wharton Risk Center during the final two years of preparation of this monograph. He labored many hours to code underlying loss data and collate it with the policy level database that formed the basis for our empirical study. The authors are deeply grateful for his assistance in this regard.

Over the several years this project has been underway, we have profited from advice and counsel of many individuals. We wish to thank especially Howard Kunreuther, whose vision and leadership in setting up and shaping the Managing Catastrophic Risks project was the foundation for this effort, and to our colleagues Georges Dionne, Neil Doherty and Richard Phillips for their constructive feedback on our research. We also recognize the great debt we owe to the Wharton Project sponsors and to insurance industry representatives for their valuable input on earlier drafts of this monograph, and especially to James Ament, David Durbin, Carl Hedde, John Kollar, and John Major for their insightful comments and constructive suggestions on this work as it developed. Our thanks also to the Russell L. Ackoff Endowment Fund for partial support of this research. While we assume full responsibility for the product of all this advice, that follows herewith, we are quite aware of the deep debt we owe these individuals for their guidance along the way in designing this study and helping us to carry it through.

Martin F. Grace
Georgia State University

Robert W. Klein
Georgia State University

Paul R. Kleindorfer
University of Pennsylvania

Michael R. Murray
Insurance Services Office, Inc.

Chapter 1

INTRODUCTION

1. THE PROBLEM OF CATASTROPHE RISK

The risk of large losses from natural disasters in the U.S. has significantly increased in recent years, straining private insurance markets and creating troublesome problems for disaster-prone areas. The threat of mega-catastrophes resulting from intense hurricanes or earthquakes striking major population centers has dramatically altered the insurance environment. Estimates of probable maximum losses (PMLs) to insurers from a mega-catastrophe striking the U.S. range up to $100 billion depending on the location and intensity of the event (Applied Insurance Research, 2001).[1] A severe disaster could have a significant financial impact on the industry (Cummins, Doherty, and Lo, 2002; Insurance Services Office, 1996a). Estimates of industry gross losses from the terrorist attack on September 11, 2001 range from $30 billion to $50 billion, and the attack's effect on insurance markets underscores the need to understand the dynamics of the supply of and the demand for insurance against extreme events, including natural disasters.

Increased catastrophe risk poses difficult challenges for insurers, reinsurers, property owners and public officials (Kleindorfer and Kunreuther, 1999). The fundamental dilemma concerns insurers' ability to handle low-probability, high-consequence (LPHC) events, which generates a host of interrelated issues with respect to how the risk of such events are

---

[1] These probable maximum loss (PML) estimates are based on a 500-year "return" period. In other words, the probability that a loss would occur in any given year that would exceed the PML is one in 500. See Appendix B for an explanation of how such PML estimates can be calculated for a given insurer's portfolio using catastrophe models.

managed, financed and priced at various levels (Russell and Jaffe, 1997). These issues became more apparent following Hurricane Andrew in 1992, the most costly natural disaster for U.S. insurers to date. In the wake of that event, insurers have sought to raise their prices to more adequate levels and decrease their exposure to catastrophe losses, while seeking more efficient ways to share their exposure through reinsurance and securitization.

However, state legislators and insurance regulators resisted insurers' efforts to raise prices and terminate policies in an attempt to preserve the availability and affordability of insurance coverage (Klein, 1998). Although insurers have been allowed to adjust their rates gradually over time, some problems still persist and there is the potential for further conflicts if assessments of catastrophe risk increase as a result of new data or improvements in catastrophe modeling.[2] Indeed, market conditions in Florida have recently started to deteriorate as regulators have halted the progression of prices to a sustainable level.[3] Regulatory restrictions have been complemented by state residual insurance mechanisms with troublesome vulnerabilities (Marlett and Eastman, 1998).

Following Hurricane Andrew, government policies imposed significant cross-subsidies from low-risk to high-risk areas and, possibly, cross-subsidies from non-catastrophe lines of insurance to the catastrophe lines. Such policies distort incentives and undermine the ability of market forces to make necessary adjustments and operate effectively in managing catastrophe risk (Grace, Klein and Kleindorfer, 1999). Hence, there is a need to inform the public and policymakers about the consequences of such actions and the potential benefits of more rational regulatory approaches.

2. OVERVIEW OF STUDY

As concerns about natural disasters have assumed center stage, researchers have begun to explore the special problems disasters pose as well as their implications for insurance markets. Understandably, recent research on catastrophe risk has focused on the topics of industry capacity, reinsurance, securitization, and hazard mitigation. Yet, much less is known about the microeconomics of catastrophe insurance markets at the primary

---

[2] For example, rates in the highest-risk coastal areas exposed to hurricanes still appear to be constrained by regulation.

[3] There have been a number of recent accounts in Florida newspapers concerning disagreements between insurers and regulators on property insurance rates. Also, the number of full-coverage policies insured through the reformed Florida residual market mechanism, the Citizen's Property Insurance Corporation, has grown from a low of residential 59,628 policies in April 2000 to 206, 256 policies as of year-end 2002, according to its latest Polices and Exposures Report (www.citizensfla.com).

level (i.e., transactions between primary insurers and individual consumers). Analyzing the supply of and demand for catastrophe insurance and integrating this analysis with research on risk diversification and mitigation is essential to formulating a more complete picture of the problems presented by catastrophe risk and evaluating potentially viable solutions. It is also critical to understanding how regulation has affected market adjustments to the new realities of catastrophe risk.

This monograph presents the results of the first significant attempt to examine the nature of the demand for insurance against natural disasters at a detailed, microeconomic level within a regulated market. Our examination has been made possible with the unprecedented assembly of an extensive, detailed database on residential insurance transactions affected by catastrophe risk.[4] These data are supplemented by public information on insurer financial and organizational characteristics and the demographic and economic characteristics of residential households at a Zip code level, as well as information on regulatory constraints on insurance rates.

We explore several significant aspects of residential insurance markets threatened by hurricanes. Our subject is the homeowners multi-peril insurance that is used to cover owner-occupied residential property. Importantly, our analysis uses a model that properly reflects the interaction of supply and demand factors to identify factors that affect consumer demand for coverage. Our work tests the statistical significance of variables thought to be key and measures their effects on the quantity, quality and price of insurance purchased. Among the phenomena we seek to illuminate are the sensitivity of demand to prices, household income and other demographic characteristics, policy features and the bundling/unbundling of perils and coverages.[5] Further, we examine insurer and consumer decisions in different market and regulatory environments – Florida and New York – over a four-year period 1995-1998.

3. SUMMARY OF FINDINGS

A number of observations arise from our analysis. Rates in high-risk coastal areas in Florida rose 100-200 percent during the decade following

---

[4] The Insurance Services Office (ISO) provided these data to the authors on a confidential basis. The insurers included in this database granted explicit permission for the authors to use these data on a confidential basis.

[5] Bundling refers to the combining of insurance against various perils for a range of coverages in a single insurance policy. Perils are causes of loss (e.g., fire, windstorm, earthquake, etc.). Coverage refers to the types of loss for which there is insurance (e.g., damage to structures, damage to contents, additional living expense, etc.).

Hurricane Andrew, reflecting the reassessment of catastrophe exposure. The availability of coverage has significantly improved since the mid-1990s, but government mechanisms were still providing coverage for the wind peril for almost 400,000 homes and full coverage for more than 200,000 dwellings as of the end of 2002. A number of homeowners insurers left the Florida market and others have entered to take their place. Insurers have adjusted the portfolios of properties they cover, but some carriers retain a high concentration of exposures in southeastern portions of the state. Deductibles, particularly for wind, have increased substantially. Insurers and insureds in New York have also experienced the effects of increased catastrophe risk, but to a much lesser degree than in Florida.[6]

Our econometric analysis focuses on factors affecting the demand for insurance, examining non-catastrophe and catastrophe coverages separately and combined. We find that the demand for catastrophe coverage is more price-sensitive than the demand for non-catastrophe coverage. This implies that public policies that reduce insurers' costs of underwriting catastrophe risk could significantly enhance the adequacy of protection against disasters purchased by homeowners.

Further, the demand for catastrophe coverage increases with income in both states. The demand for non-catastrophe coverage tends to decrease with income in New York but not Florida. When both coverages are combined, the negative income elasticity of the demand for non-catastrophe coverage dominates in New York. Overall, the demand for homeowners insurance has a low-income elasticity. This supports the theoretical literature on the relationship between income, wealth and the demand for insurance.

As expected, policy options that expand coverage generally have a positive effect on the demand for insurance and vice versa. Neighborhood and housing characteristics associated with higher risk also tend to increase demand. Interestingly, in New York, as homeowners' equity increases, their demand for non-catastrophe insurance tends to fall. Finally, regulatory suppression and compression of rates induces homeowners to buy more coverage. This may sound desirable to some, but the ultimate effect is to reduce the supply of insurance and reduce homeowners' incentives for hazard mitigation.

The monograph proceeds as follows. Chapter 2 presents an overview of the residential property insurance markets in Florida and New York. Chapter 3 discusses the regulatory framework for homeowners insurance and the regulatory policies imposed in states affected by catastrophe risk, with particular focus on Florida and New York. Chapter 4 outlines our model, the

---

[6] More recently, the severe losses caused by the terrorist attacks on September 11, 2001 have placed increased pressure on both insurers and reinsurers across the country to increase prices for all catastrophe coverage.

literature supporting it, and the hypotheses that we will test. Chapter 5 presents the results of our analysis and discusses their significance for how homeowners insurance markets function when subject to catastrophe risk and regulatory constraints. Chapter 6 concludes and summarizes our key findings.

Chapter 2

AN OVERVIEW OF CATASTROPHE INSURANCE MARKETS

Our analysis begins with an overview of the structure and performance of the catastrophe insurance markets under our microscope. We are interested in how these markets are structured in terms of the number and size distribution of insurers, entry and exit conditions, insurers' geographic concentration and the types of policies purchased by consumers. We then consider how market structure interacts with market performance in terms of pricing, profitability, availability of coverage and other dimensions. We begin with a description of the insurance products that are sold in the markets we study and the special problems that catastrophe risk imposes. We defer a discussion of the regulatory structure to Chapter 3.

1. CHARACTERISTICS OF RESIDENTIAL PROPERTY INSURANCE

Our study concentrates on the market for residential property insurance, with the primary emphasis on homeowners multi-peril insurance. Homeowners multi-peril insurance is the type of insurance most commonly used to cover owner-occupied residential properties.[1] Homeowners multi-peril insurance packages several different coverages for residential structures, their contents and inhabitants (Rejda, 2001). The perils covered typically include fire, water damage, windstorm, hail, riot, lightning, explosion, theft, and malicious mischief, as well as personal liability. Homeowners multi-peril coverage is confined to residential structures,

[1] While several property-liability insurance lines are affected by natural disasters, it is apparent that residential property insurance markets face the most significant risk and have experienced the greatest problems (see Grace, Klein and Kleindorfer, 1998).

including multi-unit structures (2-4 units), where the owner occupies one of the units.

There are several forms of homeowners multi-peril insurance that differ in terms of the perils insured and the types of losses that are covered. Box 2.1 summarizes the coverages provided under the standard Insurance Services Office (ISO) policy forms during the period of our study. The HO3 policy is the typical contract sold. It has coverages for the home and attached structures, detached structures, personal property (i.e., contents), loss of use, personal liability, and medical payments for others. The major difference between an HO3 policy and an HO5 policy is that the HO5 policy provides open-perils coverage for personal property or contents. Open-perils coverage means that there is insurance for losses due to all causes of loss except for those specifically excluded. An HO3 policy typically covers contents on a "named-perils" basis, although an HO15 endorsement can be purchased to add open-perils coverage on contents, making the combination functionally equivalent to an HO5 policy. The HO8 policy covers a less inclusive list of named perils than either HO3 or HO5 policies. HO8 policies are designed primarily for homes in older urban areas.[2]

Box 2.1

Homeowners Multi-peril Policy Provisions and Options

In Effect for Years 1996-1998

	Form			
Coverage	HO-2	HO-3	HO-5	HO-8
Dwelling (A)	Minimum varies by company.	Minimum varies by company.	Minimum varies by company.	Minimum varies by company.
Other Structures (B)	10% of A	10% of A	10% of A	10% of A
Personal Property (C)	50% of A	50% of A	50% of A	50% of A
Loss of Use (D)	20% of A	20% of A	20% of A	10% of A
Personal Liability (E)	\$100,000	\$100,000	\$100,000	\$100,000
Medical Payments (F)	\$1,000 per person	\$1,000 per person	\$1,000 per person	\$1,000 per person
Perils	Named	Open-Dwelling Named-Contents	Open	Named, Limited
Loss Settlement	RC - Dwelling ACV - Contents	RC - Dwelling ACV - Contents	RC - Dwelling ACV – Contents	RC - Dwelling ACV – Contents
Source: Insurance Services Office				

[2] HO8 policies cover a more limited set of perils than other policy forms and theft coverage is restricted to property on the premises with a limit of \$1,000.

There are also options available to cover personal property at a greater value than the standard limits, or to cover liability at a greater level than the standard limit ($100,000). Also, depending on the state and company, certain coverages may be included or excluded in a specific contract, and special endorsements may be added to provide supplemental coverage, modify standard coverage provisions, or exclude other coverages. Some of these options are discussed further below.

In coastal areas of states subject to hurricanes and tropical storms, some homeowners policies exclude damage by windstorm. Insureds can elect to exclude the wind peril to lower their premium, although this is typically not an option for insureds with a home mortgage, who are required to carry full hazard insurance. Insurers may decline to offer protection against windstorms in order to reduce their exposure to catastrophe risk. Also, in certain coastal states including Florida, when policies exclude protection against windstorms, a state residual market mechanism may offer a separate policy providing protection against windstorms.[3] The flood peril (including flooding associated with hurricanes) must be insured through a separate policy through the federal National Flood Insurance Program (NFIP).[4]

The major innovation of the homeowners multi-peril policy (which emerged in the 1960s) was the packaging of liability and property perils and the provision of broader coverage that previously had to be purchased in separate policies and policy endorsements. The concept of bundling perils and broadening coverage has driven product development over the last four decades, but the catastrophe risk problem may be prompting insurers to rethink this strategy. At the same time, consumer attitudes and regulatory restrictions may impede insurers' efforts to modify homeowners insurance policies, such as the unbundling of the wind peril in the absence of state wind pools.

Insurers have sought to modify their homeowners insurance policies in response to greater catastrophe risk. The two most noteworthy developments have been the introduction of higher deductibles for windstorm and hurricane losses and credits for hazard mitigation. Some insurers now offer separate wind deductibles that are stated percentages of the dwelling coverage limit (e.g., one, two or five percent) or a fixed amount that is higher than the deductible for other perils.

Some insurers offer premium discounts for windstorm protective devices, such as storm shutters, roof clamps, and frame tie-downs. Florida requires all insurers to offer credits for these protective devices. However, insurers are

---

3 As we will explain below, in 2002, Florida combined its wind pool and its joint underwriting association for residential property insurance into one entity.

4 Private insurers may offer earthquake coverage to homeowners, but it is unusual for a private insurer to underwrite a full non-federal flood policy for a home.

cautious about such credits because of uncertainty about the performance of windstorm protective devices and regulatory rate suppression.

Several other coverage options deserve brief mention, although they do not directly arise from catastrophe risk. These options include: 1) the policy deductible; 2) the basis of loss settlement on personal property (replacement cost or actual cash value); 3) named or open-perils coverage (discussed above); 4) additional ordinance or law coverage; and 5) alternative coverage limits. The traditional homeowners policy carries an overall deductible that applies to all property coverages and perils. This is typically a fixed dollar amount, ranging from $100-$1,000 or more, with $250-$500 being the most common. Some insurers also offer deductibles that are a stated percentage of the Coverage A (dwelling) limit for all perils. Most recently, as noted above, insurers have begun to offer separate wind deductibles in high-risk states.

Homeowners policies typically provide replacement cost coverage on the dwelling and other structures and actual cash value coverage on personal property (i.e., contents). However, homeowners may purchase replacement cost coverage on contents through a special endorsement. Ordinance or law coverage pays the additional cost (subject to stated limits) of repairing or rebuilding a dwelling according to updated and more stringent building codes than those in effect when the structure was built. Policies typically a limited amount of ordinance or law coverage, with insureds free to purchase additional amounts.

Insurers encourage or require insureds to set their Coverage A (dwelling and attached structures) limit to at least 80 percent of the value or estimated replacement cost of the insured structures.[5] The other property coverage limits are stated as percentages of the Coverage A limit. Insureds may purchase higher or lower limits than those provided in the standard policy, with corresponding adjustments in their premiums. In addition to the insured's coverage options, various rating factors are used to tailor the premium for a particular policy to the risk characteristics of the insured property.

It is also possible to purchase a more limited dwelling fire policy to cover a residential structure or its contents against certain property perils, with or without extended coverage for other perils, including windstorm (Rejda, 2001). Dwelling fire policies are less common than homeowners multi-peril

---

[5] When the Coverage A limit is less than 80 percent of the replacement value of the home, typical policy provisions allow insurers to adjust partial losses on a pro-rata basis based on the ratio of the actual limit to the value of the home. Underinsurance proved to be a chronic problem in the 1990s, and insurers have sought to encourage policyholders to raise their policy limits to adequate levels. Also, for "guaranteed" replacement cost policies, insureds are typically required to set the Coverage A limit at 100 percent of the estimated replacement cost of the dwelling.

policies and generally represent a very small portion of insured homes.[6] Because these policies remain a small and constant or declining portion of residential insurance, they do not appear to be a significant option in homeowners' choice set for insurance coverage.

2. CHALLENGES TO INSURING CATASTROPHE RISK

The risk of human and economic losses from natural disasters has grown tremendously in the U.S. within the last decade (Kunreuther, 1998a). Single-peril estimates of the maximum probable *insured* loss from one event now range up to $100 billion (AIR, 2001). The combined-peril (hurricane, earthquake, severe thunderstorm) estimated maximum probable insured loss from a single occurrence reaches $125 billion (AIR, 2001). Insurance industry assessments of catastrophe risk changed after several disasters in the early 1990s generated large insured losses. The most significant events in the U.S. (in terms of 1999 dollars of insured loss) include Hurricane Hugo ($5.7 billion) in 1989, Hurricane Andrew ($19.1 billion) in 1992; and the Northridge, California earthquake ($14.1 billion) in 1994 (Insurance Information Institute, 2001).[7]

Figure 2.1 shows the potential insured losses from a severe hurricane striking the U.S. in a heavily populated area. Based on catastrophe modeling, in a given year, there is a one percent chance of a severe hurricane with insured losses exceeding $46.4 billion (AIR, 2001).[8] There is a 0.2 percent chance of a severe hurricane with insured losses exceeding $73.8 billion. These probabilities may seem small, but one has to remember that it is a matter of "rolling the dice" every year with these odds. Hence, the probability of a severe catastrophe occurring within the next several decades is significant. Additionally, even smaller, more frequent events could cause some market disruption, and there is the possibility of more than one event occurring in any year.

---

6 Dwelling fire policies account for only about 2.6 percent of the homes insured in Florida and 0.6 percent of homes insured in New York (NAIC, 2001a).

7 Modeling companies have estimated that Hurricane Andrew would have caused $75 billion in losses if it had made landfall some 50 miles further south, striking Miami and its resort hotels on the coast directly.

8 These modeled loss estimates were provided by AIR Worldwide Corporation. The estimates cited here assume that there would be a "demand surge" phenomenon. The equivalent PMLs for the earthquake peril are $43 billion (100-year return period) and $98 billion (500-year return period). See Appendix B for AIR's explanation of these catastrophe loss estimations.

Figure 2.1
Potential Single Occurrence Hurricane Loss with Demand Surge

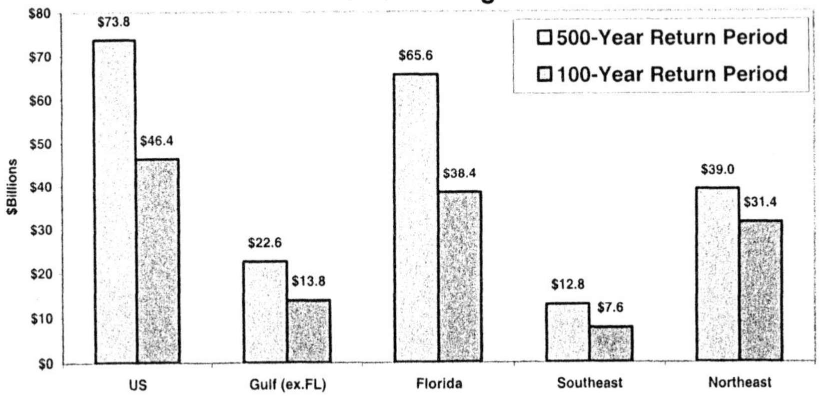

Source: Applied Insurance Research, Inc.

Also, these figures include neither significant economic losses that are not insured nor the intrinsic cost of inconvenience and the human suffering caused by natural disasters. The disasters of the late 1980s and early 1990s, combined with adverse long-term weather cycles, rapid economic growth in high-risk areas, and the availability of sophisticated modeling tools to analyze catastrophe risk, prompted insurers to reassess the potentially devastating losses that would result from mega-catastrophes.

Insurance and reinsurance markets have experienced some problems in financing and diversifying the higher layers of this risk (Froot and O'Connell, 1999).[9] These problems are reflected in the tighter supply and the increased cost of property insurance coverage in regions of the U.S. subject to natural disasters, as well as insurers' exposure to financial impairment because of catastrophes (Cummins, Doherty, and Lo, 2002; ISO, 1996a). We should note that insurers increased their capital subsequent to the disasters in the early 1990s and limits on the supply of insurance eased. However, while many insurers have increased their capacity to handle natural disasters, we do not know how far this capacity extends. It is not clear that market forces and public policy have placed a high priority on securing insurers' ability to withstand severe disasters. And, as we note below in more detail, insurance regulation has impeded insurers' adjustments to greater catastrophe risk by reducing the flexibility of insurers to curtail their exposure or increase prices

---

[9] One aspect of this problem is the intertemporal risk problem posed by catastrophes. Insurers must rely on premium flows that are relatively stable over time, but low-frequency, high-cost catastrophes require them to call on a large amount of capital to pay claims when a disaster occurs (Russell and Jaffe, 1997).

in disaster prone areas. These circumstances continue to impose some pressure on insurance markets exposed to natural disasters.

Catastrophes causing widespread devastation are inconsistent with one of the fundamental conditions distinguishing insurable risks, that is the risk of loss on different policies must be independent and diversifiable. When that condition is met, an insurer faces only a very small potential that losses from one or a series of events that will overwhelm its financial capacity (Rejda, 2001). Insurers also must be able to develop reasonably accurate estimates of their future losses so that they can set appropriate prices and structure their investments to efficiently manage their cash flows. This is very difficult to do with low-probability, high-consequence (LPHC) events that are affected by a wide range of factors and subject to considerable uncertainty.

To address these problems, many insurers now utilize sophisticated modeling techniques to measure and manage their catastrophe risk (see Appendix B for details). Reinsurers have also increasingly come to rely on these modeling techniques to assess the level of risk transferred under reinsurance contracts with primary insurers. These techniques provide a foundation for better assessment of the exposure to losses from natural disasters, and they have contributed to the recovery of catastrophe insurance markets after Hurricane Andrew. In addition to using better assessment techniques, there are several means by which insurers can manage and diversify their catastrophe risk, including: 1) reducing the geographic concentration of exposures in high risk areas; 2) modifying the terms of their insurance contracts; 3) encouraging risk mitigation; 4) purchasing reinsurance; 5) utilizing catastrophe-hedging financial instruments; 6) holding more capital; and 7) establishing catastrophe reserves.

Each of these measures involves costs and constraints on the availability of these mechanisms can hamper insurers' efforts to manage and cover catastrophe losses. Insurers lose certain administrative efficiencies when they reduce their concentration of exposures. Contract modifications that lower an insurer's risk may be undesirable to consumers. Risk mitigation requires up-front financial investments with long-term payoffs that may be undervalued by homeowners and housing markets.[10] Reinsurance can be relatively expensive, and there are ultimately some constraints on reinsurers' ability to assume a significant amount of catastrophe risk, particularly at higher layers. The market for catastrophe-hedging instruments is still in its infancy, and buyers have demanded a high-risk premium because of their lack of familiarity with catastrophe risk and uncertainty about the likelihood

[10] Insurers are somewhat reluctant to offer significant premium discounts for mitigation when regulators prevent them from charging adequate rates.

that these instruments will be triggered.[11] Statutory and GAAP accounting principles do not currently provide for reserves for future catastrophes and such reserves are subject to taxation (Davidson, 1996).[12] Harrington and Niehaus (2001) demonstrate that there is a very high tax cost to setting aside capital for future catastrophe losses.[13] Thus, under current tax law and regulatory policies, accumulating additional capital to finance future catastrophe losses is costly. Further, if insurers accumulate additional capital to fund catastrophe losses, this capital is subject to expropriation through corporate takeovers or regulation.

Despite these problems, there is some reason to believe that the pressure on catastrophe insurance markets has at least temporarily moderated in the last several years. Insurers were gradually allowed to raise their prices and adjust their exposures somewhat, and prices may be closer to sustainable levels today than they were in the years immediately following Hurricane Andrew. Additional capacity flowed into the reinsurance market to respond to primary insurers' demand for catastrophe coverage. For the most part, since the early 1990s, insurers and property owners have dodged the bullet of a major hurricane and the resulting losses, which has further assisted the recovery of the market and the accumulation of additional funds (subject to accounting rules and tax law).

Still, we should not become sanguine about the potential threat of severe catastrophes. While insurers may be better positioned to absorb the loss shock from a moderate catastrophe (e.g., less than $50 billion), a severe catastrophe could still devastate the industry, causing substantial financial impairment and market disruption (Cummins, Doherty, and Lo, 2002). Further, the tragic events of September 11, 2001 indicate that natural disasters are not the only potential source of catastrophe loss shocks to insurers' and reinsurers' capital.[14] In the face of these looming threats,

---

[11] See Grace, Klein and Phillips (2001) for a discussion of the use of Special Purpose Reinsurance Vehicles (SPRVs) to facilitate securitization of catastrophe risk. See Kunreuther and Bantwell (2000) for a discussion of the structure of securitization vehicles for catastrophe risks, and some possible reasons for the large price differentials for these vehicles relative to other financial instruments with similar risk/default characteristics.

[12] Russell and Jaffee (1997) point out that insurers' inability to set aside catastrophe reserves to fund infrequent, but severe losses from natural disasters is a major problem. Under current accounting rules, insurers have to accumulate additional capital to fund future catastrophe losses that is subject to expropriation.

[13] In the U.S., unlike the situation in Europe and elsewhere around the world, insurers are not permitted to establish reserves for future catastrophe losses on a tax-deferred basis. Some have advocated that U.S. taxation be changed to allow tax-deferred catastrophe reserves.

[14] In the wake of September 11, many reinsurers have opted to limit or exclude coverage for losses due to terrorism from the reinsurance contracts they offer primary insurers. See Kunreuther (2002) for a discussion. In November 2002, President Bush signed the Terrorism Risk Insurance Act of 2002 into law. That law provides a federal reinsurance

prudence suggests that we use the time we have to evaluate how catastrophe insurance markets are functioning and consider how we might further enhance their efficiency and resilience.

3. MARKET STRUCTURE

3.1 Market Concentration

Concentration is an important aspect of insurance market structure, both in terms of its potential effect on competition and market performance, and its implications for insurers' vulnerability to severe losses from a catastrophe or series of catastrophes. On the one hand, less concentration may be advantageous in promoting greater competition as well as greater risk diversification. On the other hand, greater concentration can facilitate increased economic efficiency if low-cost insurers are able to write a larger share of the market and also reap administrative savings from servicing a greater number of policies in a given geographic area.

We measure market concentration using concentration ratios at the four-firm (CR4), eight-firm (CR8), and 20-firm (CR20) levels and the Herfindahl-Hirschman Index (HHI). A concentration ratio is equal to the combined market share of some number of the top insurers, e.g., CR4 is equal to the combined market share of the top four insurers. The HHI is equal to the sum of the squared market shares of all firms in the market and can range from near zero to 10,000 (the HHI value when there is only one firm in the market with a 100% market share). Higher values of these indices indicate higher market concentration. These measures reflect the potential market power possessed by the largest firms in a market as well as their share of the risk covered by insurance.[15] Note that concentration is principally measured using data for groups of affiliated insurers and non-affiliated, stand-alone insurers, which better reflects the implications of concentration for competition. We should also note that acquisitions and

---

backstop for commercial insurance markets but provides no such backstop for personal insurance markets. Absent the availability of private reinsurance or a federal terrorism reinsurance mechanism for personal insurance, primary insurers have sought the option to exclude coverage for losses due to terrorism from the policies they offer, but state regulators have declined to approve such exclusions.

[15] These concentration measures are somewhat crude indicators of catastrophe risk exposure as they are based on statewide data on premiums written. An insurer's market share could vary significantly among different areas within a state with different degrees of catastrophe risk.

mergers of insurance companies and groups affect all of our measures of market structure.[16]

Table 2.1 shows the number of insurers and market concentration measures for homeowners insurance for Florida, New York and countrywide. Three data points were chosen – 1992, 1995 and 2000. The data for these years indicate how market concentration has changed since Hurricane Andrew in 1992.

In Florida, the number of insurer groups dropped from 122 in 1992 to 100 in 1995 and then rose to 114 by 2000. Analogously, market concentration increased during the first part of the decade and then fell by 2000. The HHI was 1,238 in 1992, rose to 1,406 in 1995, and then dropped to 772 in 2000. This is consistent with how insurers would be expected to respond to Hurricane Andrew and the regulatory policies that followed. Over time, as insurers have been able to gradually adjust their rates and portfolios of exposures, the number of firms serving the market has bounced back. Also, as discussed below, market conditions attracted some new insurers that were in a position to cover homes exposed to catastrophe risk and utilize the state's residual market depopulation program. Overall, the degree of market concentration in Florida is relatively low and is consistent with a competitive market structure.

New York presents a different pattern in terms of time trends. The number of insurer groups steadily dropped from 131 in 1992 to 113 in 2000. In turn, market concentration increased, but not by much and not to a level that would raise concerns about competition. The HHI was 653 in 1992 and 737 in 2000. The factors appearing to influence the structure of New York's market differ from those affecting Florida's. Insurers also have been concerned about catastrophe risk in coastal areas of New York, but the nature of this risk differs from that in Florida. New York tends to receive less intense tropical storms, although the value of property exposed to storms is high. Importantly, winter storms (Nor'easters) are a problem, although they pack less catastrophe potential than hurricanes. Also, other homeowners perils, such as fire, theft and liability, could be more significant in New York than in Florida. The reason for the decline of the number of homeowners insurers in New York remains an open question and may be more reflective of national trends than state-specific factors.

Market concentration at a countrywide level is important, not only in providing a basis for comparison, but because of its potential implications

[16] For example, suppose an insurer group did not write any homeowners insurance in Florida in 1992, but subsequently acquired an insurer group that did write homeowners insurance in Florida in 1992. In our analysis, we would show the acquired insurer as exiting the market and the acquiring insurer as entering the market.

for state markets.[17] The countrywide pattern differs from the patterns in both Florida and New York. The number of insurer groups providing homeowners insurance increased from 477 in 1992 to 531 in 1995 and then fell to 476 in 2000. But, based on HHIs, countrywide market concentration steadily decreased, with the HHI falling from 926 in 1992 to 758 in 2000.

The drop in the number of insurers writing homeowners insurance may be caused by several factors, including adverse catastrophe experience, the poor profitability of the line due to intense competition, and others. That the HHI for homeowners dropped even as the number of insurers writing homeowners declined indicates that there has been a redistribution of business among the remaining suppliers, with the largest insurers ceding some market share to other insurers.

TABLE 2.1

Number of Insurers and Market Concentration
Florida, New York and Countrywide
1992, 1995, and 2000

State/Year	Direct Prem Written	Number of Insurers		Concentration Indicators (Group Basis)			
		Companies	Groups	CR4	CR8	CR20	HHI
Florida							
1992	1,169,849,229	234	122	54.7%	66.5%	81.9%	1,238
1995	1,684,973,701	202	100	60.2%	72.2%	87.4%	1,406
2000	2,907,309,923	223	114	47.9%	61.0%	78.4%	772
New York							
1992	1,701,051,571	224	131	42.8%	56.0%	78.9%	653
1995	1,959,668,327	219	125	45.7%	58.4%	82.2%	689
2000	2,331,288,562	212	113	47.9%	63.9%	85.2%	737
Countrywide							
1992	14,850,374,028	889	477	45.5%	53.6%	68.1%	926
1995	26,035,498,521	1,008	531	44.7%	54.8%	69.4%	804
2000	34,710,439,198	1,029	476	46.0%	57.9%	74.0%	758

Source: NAIC Financial Database

3.2 Entry and Exit

Some further insight into market structure can be gained by looking at the entry and exit conditions. The extent of entry and exit barriers are important factors in the competitive structure of a market. Ease of entry allows new firms to enter a market and impose competitive pressure on incumbent firms. Indeed, even in a highly concentrated market, the threat of entry can discipline firms in the market. The cost of exit also is important because it can discourage firms from entering a market. Further, conditions that

[17] Insurers operating at a national level can enter a particular state if market conditions warrant it.

encourage insurers' entrance into catastrophe-prone markets can facilitate a broader diversification of this risk.

It is difficult to quantify entry and exit barriers, but we can offer some qualitative observations as well as analyze data on actual entries and exits. Fixed minimum regulatory capital requirements for multi-line property-casualty stock insurers range from $500,000 to $6 million among the states, with the median around $2 million (Klein, 2000). The risk-based capital (RBC) requirement for a typical insurer is higher than this, but not high enough to be a substantial entry deterrent (Klein, 2000). Also, new and growing insurers can use reinsurance to boost their capacity.

Information, expertise, distribution outlets, reputation and customer relationships probably have a greater effect on entry. Information and expertise can be particularly important for proper pricing and underwriting in markets subject to catastrophe risk or that present other special circumstances. Personal lines insurers employ an array of distribution systems, some involving higher fixed costs (e.g., exclusive agents) and others involving higher variable costs (e.g., independent agents). Some insurers have invested heavily in marketing and developing a reputation with consumers. The significance of these entry costs or barriers probably depends on the segment of a market that an entrant is seeking to penetrate. For example, competing against well-known, direct writers for preferred risks could be a more challenging proposition than marketing to high-risk insureds served by non-standard carriers or government facilities.

With respect to the actual frequency of entries and exits, we would expect to see at least a small number of insurers both entering and exiting a workably competitive market over time. Insurers that fail to respond to buyer needs efficiently and with reasonable profits would be expected to leave the market. New insurers entering the market can help respond to growing demand, promote innovation, lower prices and pressure incumbent firms to improve. However, markets subject to a high level of catastrophe risk present a special challenge. Entry can be discouraged by restrictive regulation, and exit impeded by exit barriers.[18] On the other hand, some entrants may be encouraged by the opportunity to write homeowners who have been terminated by other insurers, which helps to maintain the availability of insurance.

We know from Table 2.1 that the number of insurers has decreased countrywide. At the same time, some new insurers have entered the market, presumably to take advantage of opportunities created by insurers exiting or

---

[18] One way in which regulators can impose an exit barrier is by requiring an insurer to exit all lines of business in a state if it wishes to exit a particular line, such as homeowners or auto insurance. Other ways include restrictions on insurers' freedom to cancel or non-renew policies.

reducing their business. Further, some insurer groups may be redistributing business among their affiliated companies for strategic reasons. This includes the redistribution of high-risk exposures within a group to companies with more appropriate rate structures.[19] Also, some insurers have transferred business to single-state affiliates.

Table 2.2 provides data on entries and exits for Florida, New York and countrywide. In Florida, we can see that exits outpaced entries from 1992 to 1995 in response to Hurricane Andrew, but then turned around with entries outpacing exits from 1995 to 2000. The relative frequency of entry and exit activity has been high. This probably reflects "a changing of the guard" as insurers concerned about high catastrophe exposure and/or poor experience have retrenched or left and other insurers have decided to try their hand, possibly attracted by the potential for high income in years with low catastrophe losses or the opportunity to earn reasonable profits over a number of years.

TABLE 2.2

Entries and Exits in Homeowners Insurance Markets
Insurer Groups: 1992-2000

	1995-2000						1992-1995						Number of Insurers		
	Entries		Exits		Net Change		Entries		Exits		Net Change				
State/Test	No.	Pct.	No.	Pct.	No.	Pct.	No.	Pct.	No.	Pct.	No.	Pct.	1992	1995	2000
Florida															
Test 1	48	48.0%	34	34.0%	14	14.0%	16	13.1%	38	31.1%	-22	-18.0%	122	100	114
Test 2	44	50.0%	33	37.5%	11	12.5%	14	13.9%	27	26.7%	-13	-12.9%	101	88	99
New York															
Test 1	26	20.8%	38	30.4%	-12	-9.6%	19	14.6%	24	18.5%	-5	-3.8%	130	125	113
Test 2	22	20.6%	31	29.0%	-9	-8.4%	16	15.0%	16	15.0%	0	0.0%	107	107	98
Countrywide															
Test 1	126	23.7%	181	34.1%	-55	-10.4%	133	27.9%	79	16.6%	54	11.3%	477	531	476
Test 2	123	25.2%	167	34.2%	-44	-9.0%	129	29.9%	71	16.5%	58	13.5%	431	489	445

Test 1: Insurer is considered "in the market" if it has direct premiums written > 0 in a given year.
Test 2: Insurer is considered "in the market" if it has direct premiums written >$100,000 in a given year.
Source: NAIC Financial Database

In New York, exits were greater than entries during both periods, particularly over the last half of the decade. At the same time, the relative movement of firms in New York (in terms of entries/exits in relation to the total number of firms) has been somewhat lower in New York than in Florida. This suggests that the factors affecting entry and exit were more long-term in New York and, possibly, that regulation in New York posed fewer problems for insurers.

Countrywide, entries were greater than exits from 1992 to 1995 and vice versa from 1995 to 2000. This is an interesting pattern that warrants further

[19] Each company within a group must file and obtain approval for its own rates. The different companies within a group may have different rate structures – lower rates for low-risk insureds and higher rates for high-risk insureds.

investigation. Homeowners insurance may have appeared to be an attractive line for entry in the mid-1990s, at least in states with a low catastrophe exposure. Profits in these states may have appeared to be relatively high, a strong motivation for entry. Also, some insurers may have perceived a potential to cross-market different insurance products to homeowners insurance customers. Subsequently, aggressive price competition combined with adverse experience may have caused a number of insurers to exit this line in the latter part of the decade.[20]

TABLE 2.3a

Changes in Leading Insurers' Market Share
Florida - 1992, 1995, 2000

	2000			1995			1992		
Name	Rank	DPW	MS	Rank	DPW	MS	Rank	DPW	MS
State Farm Group	1	583,296,400	20.1%	1	523,718,334	31.1%	1	326,713,656	27.9%
Hannover Group	2	330,849,854	11.4%						
Allstate Group	3	325,641,465	11.2%	2	293,679,212	17.4%	2	218,164,808	18.6%
USAA Group	4	152,088,271	5.2%	4	91,130,417	5.4%	3	47,585,509	4.1%
Nationwide	5	144,675,744	5.0%	5	80,912,210	4.8%	4	44,297,434	3.8%
Citigroup	6	92,445,712	3.2%	3	106,697,390	6.3%	88	377,189	0.0%
Hartford Fire & Casualty Group	7	76,738,521	2.6%	6	43,881,208	2.6%	10	24,644,122	2.1%
Chubb & Son	8	68,324,921	2.4%	11	31,015,810	1.8%	7	31,437,455	2.7%
Southern Farm Bureau Casualty	9	59,636,471	2.1%	7	41,734,567	2.5%			
Liberty Mutual Group	10	51,714,570	1.8%	12	28,536,397	1.7%	13	16,267,496	1.4%
Florida Select Holdings Group	11	51,366,669	1.8%						
Frontier Insurance Group	12	46,571,365	1.6%						
Maguire Corporation Group	13	42,295,949	1.5%						
Allianz Insurance Group	14	41,828,548	1.4%	13	27,680,518	1.6%	15	11,658,623	1.0%
American International Group	15	38,442,829	1.3%	21	9,557,402	0.6%	60	1,879,275	0.2%
Poe Financial Group	16	38,322,429	1.3%						
Bankers Insurance Group	17	34,447,462	1.2%	53	2,313,052	0.1%	75	917,162	0.1%
Prudential of America Group	18	34,274,837	1.2%	8	35,081,722	2.1%	5	39,925,717	3.4%
American Superior Insurance Company	19	33,911,175	1.2%						
Qualsure Insurance Corporation	20	32,749,248	1.1%						

Source: NAIC Financial Database

Looking at shifts among the leading insurer groups may offer some further insights. Tables 2.3(a)-2.3(c) reveal changes in the amount of direct premiums written by leading insurer groups from 1992 to 2000. In Table 2.3(a), we can see that there has been a significant amount of turnover among the leading insurers in Florida. There has been little change among the top five insurers, but many changes beyond the top five. Among the leading 20 insurers in 2000, seven were not even in the market in 1995. The new insurers include the Hannover Group, Florida Select, the Frontier Insurance Group, the Maguire Corporation Group, the Poe Financial Group, American Superior Insurance Company, and Qualsure Insurance Corporation. Also, Bankers Insurance Group rose from 75th in 1992 to 17th in 2000. Some insurers have significantly retrenched and reduced their share

[20] Indeed, the supply of homeowners insurance tightened in many states in 2001 and 2002, due to several factors, including substantial net losses suffered by insurers in the late 1990s.

of the market while others have moved up. These changes could result from active strategies by some insurers to significantly alter their writings and risk exposures as other insurers implemented "stay the course" strategies. Also, we must remember that entries and exits, as well as market growth or retrenchment, may occur through the sale, acquisition and merger of insurance companies and groups.

TABLE 2.3b

Changes in Leading Insurers' Market Share
New York - 1992, 1995, 2000

Name	2000			1995			1992		
	Rank	DPW	MS	Rank	DPW	MS	Rank	DPW	MS
Allstate Group	1	410,220,916	17.6%	1	342,360,967	17.5%	1	312,234,515	18.4%
State Farm Group	2	291,351,435	12.5%	2	238,816,678	12.2%	2	184,482,522	10.8%
Citigroup	3	226,196,680	9.7%	3	189,063,941	9.6%			
Chubb & Son	4	188,089,673	8.1%	4	124,908,913	6.4%	4	104,370,519	6.1%
Nationwide	5	97,318,729	4.2%	5	73,157,148	3.7%	7	49,230,431	2.9%
Central Services Group	6	94,271,385	4.0%	6	60,405,197	3.1%	9	46,692,009	2.7%
CGU Insurance Group	7	92,444,264	4.0%	14	41,058,401	2.1%	18	26,272,630	1.5%
Liberty Mutual Group	8	89,860,596	3.9%	7	59,138,176	3.0%	8	46,884,089	2.8%
CNA Insurance Group	9	58,294,659	2.5%	9	55,316,740	2.8%	13	34,850,356	2.0%
Metropolitan Group	10	57,531,803	2.5%	11	48,654,462	2.5%	14	33,450,523	2.0%
Hartford Fire & Casualty Group	11	57,250,285	2.5%	10	54,238,114	2.8%	10	45,213,147	2.7%
Royal & Sun Alliance America	12	48,543,752	2.1%						
Allianz Insurance Group	13	45,671,946	2.0%	17	30,511,152	1.6%	19	21,811,889	1.3%
Prudential of America Group	14	43,936,579	1.9%	12	43,213,180	2.2%	12	34,923,262	2.1%
USAA Group	15	43,801,541	1.9%	16	31,989,015	1.6%	17	26,802,370	1.6%
Lumbermens Mutual Casualty Group	16	34,449,531	1.5%	20	26,213,417	1.3%	22	20,669,811	1.2%
AllAmerica Financial Corporation	17	30,239,002	1.3%	19	26,289,266	1.3%	16	27,009,181	1.6%
St. Paul Group	18	29,895,399	1.3%	40	6,486,873	0.3%	47	4,308,119	0.3%
Utica National Insurance Group	19	23,543,409	1.0%	24	18,016,456	0.9%	32	11,151,134	0.7%
Amica Mutual Group	20	23,397,989	1.0%	21	19,754,563	1.0%	26	17,643,547	1.0%

Source: NAIC Financial Database

New start-up companies, partially capitalized by a $100 bounty for every Florida JUA policy, assumed many of the policies taken from the JUA. As would be expected, these insurers have acquired a high concentration of exposures in high-risk coastal areas of Florida. The data indicate, that the larger a company's homeowners' market share in Florida, the lower it's A.M. Best rating is likely to be. This may be partly attributable to Best's concern about companies with a high concentration of homeowners business in Florida, but it also may reflect lower capitalization for small and start-up companies that have a disproportionate share of the Florida homeowners market.

As a result of Florida's regulatory policies with respect to catastrophe insurance pricing and underwriting restrictions, certain insurers have sought to insulate their nationwide operations by setting up Florida-only subsidiaries.[21] The Florida subsidiary could be dissolved in the case of a

---

[21] This same approach has been used in other problem markets, such as auto insurance in New Jersey.

catastrophe without taxing the parent, as long as the legal formalities of incorporation are observed and no fraud occurs.[22] Also, the effects of market conditions and regulation in a particular state are more apparent in a single-state subsidiary. This may help to encourage reasonable regulatory policies.

TABLE 2.3c

Changes in Leading Insurers' Market Share
Countrywide - 1992, 1995, 2000

Name	2000			1995			1992		
	Rank	DPW	MS	Rank	DPW	MS	Rank	DPW	MS
State Farm Group	1	7,530,049,063	21.7%	1	6,201,238,140	23.8%	1	4,933,032,138	26.0%
Allstate Group	2	3,971,989,818	11.4%	2	3,039,452,009	11.7%	2	2,579,597,475	13.6%
Zurich Insurance Group	3	2,899,188,454	8.4%	41	97,181,684	0.4%	29	114,769,439	0.6%
Nationwide	4	1,552,982,843	4.5%	6	813,079,027	3.1%	171	7,296,474	0.0%
Citigroup	5	1,300,140,917	3.7%	5	829,245,519	3.2%	139	10,965,232	0.1%
USAA Group	6	1,234,487,566	3.6%	4	865,569,615	3.3%	3	637,493,938	3.4%
Chubb & Son	7	834,870,607	2.4%	7	522,953,585	2.0%	4	474,753,038	2.5%
Safeco Insurance Group	8	756,897,305	2.2%	9	440,521,214	1.7%	10	311,102,063	1.6%
American Family Insurance Group	9	734,601,460	2.1%	11	411,113,038	1.6%	9	313,089,556	1.7%
Liberty Mutual Group	10	712,978,496	2.1%	13	374,001,693	1.4%	11	289,991,265	1.5%
Hartford Fire & Casualty Group	11	573,855,680	1.7%	12	407,239,033	1.6%	8	326,542,587	1.7%
CNA Insurance Group	12	480,070,950	1.4%	10	420,174,639	1.6%	44	66,430,435	0.4%
CGU Insurance Group	13	455,848,463	1.3%	19	222,175,026	0.9%	24	144,768,497	0.8%
Prudential of America Group	14	439,912,058	1.3%	8	474,713,642	1.8%	6	414,252,212	2.2%
Metropolitan Group	15	411,429,272	1.2%	14	288,667,973	1.1%	18	187,706,188	1.0%
Allianz Insurance Group	16	400,264,815	1.2%	16	281,525,024	1.1%	27	133,709,505	0.7%
Auto Owners Group	17	376,510,166	1.1%	20	209,357,700	0.8%	21	165,658,689	0.9%
Hannover Group	18	362,269,745	1.0%						
Erie Insurance Group	19	354,971,422	1.0%	22	195,423,856	0.8%	26	135,220,876	0.7%
AllAmerica Financial Corporation	20	308,361,240	0.9%	17	246,042,902	0.9%	15	204,051,087	1.1%

Source: NAIC Financial Database

Table 2.3(d) provides some further indication of the movement of business among companies within the leading groups in Florida. This table shows the distribution of direct written premiums among individual companies within the 10 leading groups in 1999. We can see the formation of single-state companies within several of the leading groups, including State Farm Florida Insurance Company, Allstate Floridian Indemnity Corporation, Allstate Floridian Insurance Company, and First Floridian Auto and Home Insurance Company (Citigroup). These companies have assumed a major portion of the Florida business of their respective groups. Other shifts reflect attempts to better align exposures with the underwriting and rating structures of different companies within a group.

---

[22] This does not imply that a group would necessarily abandon a single-state insurer if its surplus was exhausted by a catastrophe, but the group would be in a position to make a strategic decision as to whether it was in the group's interest to bail out the subsidiary. Allowing a state-specific subsidiary to go insolvent could cause irreparable damage to the image of the surviving members of the group and, hence, would likely be undertaken only as a last resort in an extreme situation.

TABLE 2.3d
Changes Within Leading Groups
Florida - 1992, 1995, 1999

CNAME	DPW99	R99	DPW95	R95	DPW92	R92
State Farm Group						
STATE FARM FIRE AND CAS CO	132,983,297	4	504,823,127	1	308,437,267	1
STATE FARM FLORIDA INS CO	441,087,638	1	0	NA	0	NA
STATE FARM GENERAL INS CO	7,915,426	56	18,895,207	17	18,276,389	9
Hannover Group						
CLARENDON NATL INS CO	142,284,834	3	16,942,944	21	0	NA
CLARENDON SELECT INS CO	131,465,477	5	0	NA	0	NA
HARBOR SPECIALTY INS CO	33,523,496	17	0	NA	0	NA
Allstate Group						
ALLSTATE FLORIDIAN INDEMNITY CORP	9,646,749	49	0	NA	0	NA
ALLSTATE FLORIDIAN INSURANCE CO	305,989,911	2	0	NA	0	NA
ALLSTATE IND CO	-18,862	NA	13,974,666	22	11,233,440	17
ALLSTATE INS CO	-320,300	NA	279,704,546	2	206,931,368	2
USAA Group						
UNITED SERVICES AUTO ASSOC	99,466,912	7	68,428,873	4	37,873,610	5
USAA CAS INS CO	42,795,232	11	22,701,544	13	9,711,899	19
Nationwide Group						
NATIONWIDE MUT FIRE INS CO	121,735,574	6	78,843,286	3	43,775,200	3
SCOTTSDALE INS CO	11,719,847	43	2,068,924	79	522,231	129
Citigroup						
AUTOMOBILE INS CO OF HARTFORD CT	2,705,717	96	28,679,065	8	11,111,540	18
CHARTER OAK FIRE INS CO	76,633	181	2,998,738	62	3,515,129	56
FIRST FLORIDIAN AUTO & HOME INS CO	63,702,762	8	0	NA	0	NA
GULF UNDERWRITERS INS CO	1,454,378	115	0	NA	0	NA
PHOENIX INS CO	3,176,140	89	17,477,117	20	14,324,151	15
STANDARD FIRE INS CO	4,076,158	76	33,479,098	6	15,386,380	12
TRAVELERS IND CO	1,383,431	118	22,321,060	14	14,830,973	13
TRAVELERS IND CO OF AMER	2,430,112	99	1,743,390	87	943,320	101
Hartford Fire & Casualty Group						
HARTFORD CAS INS CO	6,279,727	67	4,197,539	49	2,790,384	66
HARTFORD FIRE IN CO	11,364,049	44	5,773,400	38	497,332	133
HARTFORD INS CO OF THE MIDWEST	38,477,996	13	21,025,107	16	11,474,208	16
HARTFORD INS CO OF THE SOUTHEAST	9,457,292	50	8,139,404	29	6,207,506	29
HARTFORD UNDERWRITERS INS CO	395,705	152	389,851	131	429,232	135
TWIN CITY FIRE INS CO CO	3,596,842	83	4,355,907	48	3,245,460	59
Chubb & Son Group						
CHUBB CUSTOM INS CO	3,363,139	85	680,410	120	214,457	161
FEDERAL INS CO	44,386,214	10	22,936,310	11	23,062,515	6
GREAT NORTHERN INS CO	6,347,904	64	5,816,369	37	6,346,154	27
VIGILANT INS CO	1,207,357	125	1,331,810	94	1,589,195	82
Southern Farm Bureau Group						
FLORIDA FARM BUREAU CAS INS CO	29,260,876	20	18,578,858	18	6,866,533	26
FLORIDA FARM BUREAU GENERAL INS CO	27,918,278	23	23,155,863	10	0	NA
SOUTHERN FARM BUREAU CAS INS CO	0	NA	-154	NA	1,781,096	77
Liberty Mutual Group						
FIRST LIBERTY INS CORP	2,841,265	94	294,616	137	0	NA
LIBERTY MUT FIRE INS CO	45,498,408	9	28,241,781	9	16,267,496	11

Source: NAIC Financial Database

In New York (Table 2.3(b)), we see much greater stability among the leading insurer groups over the decade. Of the 20 leading groups in 2000, 14 were among the 20 leading groups in 1992. There were two notable additions to the top 20 for 2000: Citigroup (which acquired and, subsequently, spun-off Travelers) and Royal & Sun Alliance (the product of a merger). New York's greater stability is probably reflective of the long-term commitment of some insurers to the New York market. Upstate New York's lower exposure to catastrophe risk and, possibly, differences in the state's regulatory climate, may have contributed to this commitment and stability. Also, the changes that have occurred in New York are likely more aligned with certain aspects of the national restructuring of the homeowners insurance market.

Interestingly, when we examine shifts among the leading homeowners insurers countrywide, we see less stability than in the New York market, although not the level of turnover in the Florida market. There are several notable changes. Zurich, Nationwide and Citigroup moved from relatively low rankings in 1992, to become the 3rd, 4th, and 5th largest writers in 2000. Also, the Hannover Group reported no homeowners premiums in 1992 and 1995, but by 1999 it had acquired a 1 percent market share and was ranked 18th. It should be noted that mergers and acquisitions played a major role in some of these changes, such as the Citicorp/Travelers merger.

In sum, these trends indicate the dynamic nature of the homeowners insurance market and its vitality. Some insurers have retrenched or left the market. At the same time, other insurers have moved in to take the place of those that left and expand their business. Ultimately, this promotes market efficiency and a continuing supply of coverage, albeit with some consumers needing to change carriers.

3.3 Geographic Concentration of Insurers

The location and geographic distribution of the business written by an insurer has an important affect on the amount of catastrophe risk the insurer faces. Insurers with exposures broadly spread (geographically) are less vulnerable to severe losses from one event. Insurers with a concentration of exposures in high-risk areas are more vulnerable and must use other means to manage and diversify their risk, such as reinsurance and securitization.

The Florida Insurance Department collects exposure data by county and by insurer that allow us to assess each insurer's distribution of exposures among Florida counties. For each company, we calculated geographic HHI values based on the percentage of their exposures in each county in 1996 and 2001. We divided the insurers into quartiles and show the un-weighted and weighted company mean values for each quartile and all insurers combined in Figures 2.2(a)–2.2(b).

Figure 2.2(a)
Insurer Geographic Concentration: Florida
Un-Weighted Mean Company HHI by Quartile

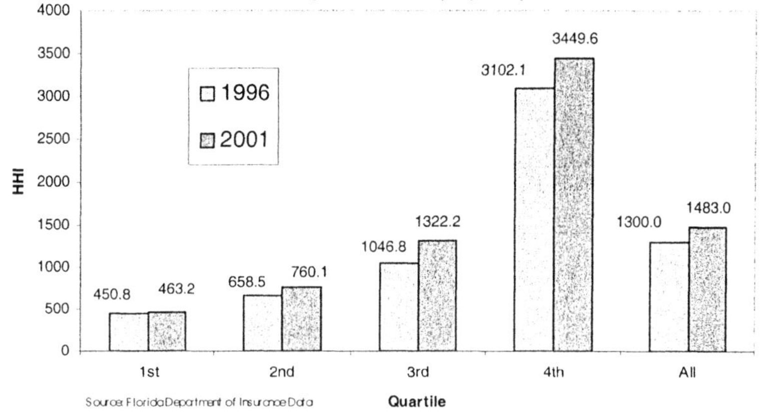

Figure 2.2(b)
Insurer Geographic Concentration: Florida
Weighted Mean Company HHI by Quartile

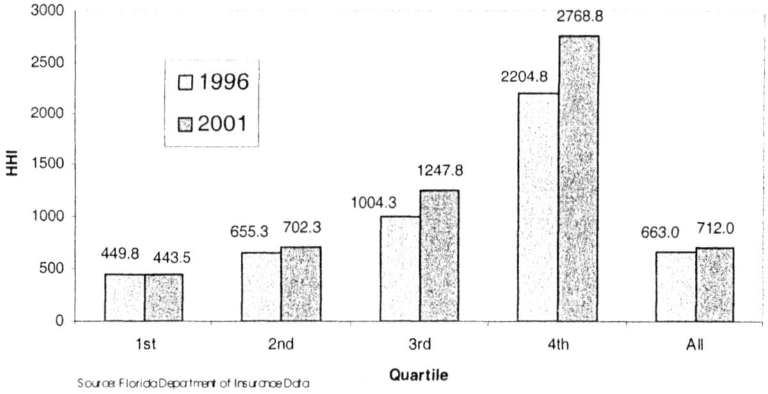

Interestingly, this analysis indicates that insurers' distributions of exposures became more skewed from 1996 to 2001 (i.e., their HHI values increased). The un-weighted mean HHI (for all insurers) increased from 1,300 to 1,483 and the weighted mean increased from 663 to 712. The mean HHI increased more in the higher quartiles, in both absolute and relative terms. For example, the weighted mean HHI for the fourth quartile increased from 2,205 in 1996 to 2,769 in 2001 or 25.6 percent. It appears that most insurers are broadly spread across the state, but a significant minority of insurers are concentrated in certain areas.

Some of these insurers are concentrated in low-risk areas while others are concentrated in high-risk areas, such as the southeast coast. The latter group includes insurers that took policies out of the JUA, which had a large number of exposures in coastal areas. Other insurers may be geographically concentrated because of their market orientation and spatial economies.[23] Regulators need to ensure that companies with high concentrations of exposures in high-risk areas have strategies and are taking steps to diversify their risk geographically and/or through financial mechanisms. This may take some time for newer companies and market entrants.

3.4 Changes in Contracts Purchased

Finally, we look at the distribution of policy forms and provisions among insureds in our transaction-level database. Table 2.4 shows this distribution in Florida and New York for 1995 and 1998. This analysis is interesting because it reveals the coverages purchased by homeowners and how they changed from 1995 to 1998.

In Florida, we can see that HO3 policies greatly predominate, representing 94.2 percent of all policies in our sample in 1998. Note that these are HO3 policies without an HO15 endorsement. HO5 (and HO3/HO15 policies which we classify as HO5 policies) constituted 5.5 percent of all policies in 1998. HO3 policies increased from 91.9 percent in 1995 and HO5 policies decreased from 8.1 percent in 1995. This suggests that some insureds with HO5 policies shifted to HO3 policies over this period, perhaps as a means to moderate increases in their premiums.

The distribution of certain policy provisions is even more dynamic. In Florida, Coverage A limits generally increased, which is likely due to rising home values and, possibly, an increase of policy limits relative to home value.[24] The shift in deductibles, particularly for wind, was more dramatic. We converted percentage deductibles to dollar amounts to place all deductibles on a comparable basis. In 1995, 69.2 percent of policies had wind deductibles between \$100 and \$250. By 1998, 43.4 percent were in the \$251-\$500 range and another 43.4 percent were in excess of \$1,000.[25] If insurers offered significant discounts or other inducements for higher wind

---

[23] Spatial economies refer to the efficiencies gained from serving a larger number of policyholders who are geographically proximate. This could lower the average expense per policy in terms of underwriting, distribution, advertising and adjusting claims.

[24] The latter development could have been prompted by insureds' desire to ensure that their policy limits more fully covered the value of their property, as well as insurers' diligence in encouraging adequate limits.

[25] Several things may have occurred. Some insureds may have increased their fire and wind deductibles by the same amount. Other homeowners likely opted for higher fixed or percentage wind deductibles, which tend to result in higher deductible levels measured in dollars. Also, if the policy limit increased with a given percentage deductible, the deductible would increase in dollar terms.

deductibles, it appears that homeowners strongly responded to these inducements to moderate their premiums and retain coverage. Changes in other policy provisions were negligible. Very few insureds appear to have wind excluded from their policies, and most carry replacement cost on contents and additional ordinance/law coverage.

Table 2.4
Homeowners Insurance Policy Provisions

Florida											
Policy Form			Policy Limits			Fire Deductibles			Wind Deductibles		
	Freq. Dist.			Freq. Dist.			Freq. Dist.			Freq. Dist.	
Type	1995	1998	Type	1995	1998	Type	1995	1998	Type	1995	1998
HO-2	0.6%	0.3%	≤100T	45.4%	38.7%	100-250	75.0%	43.9%	100-250	69.2%	4.6%
HO-3	91.9%	94.2%	101T-200T	42.5%	48.7%	251-500	20.8%	46.6%	251-500	19.8%	43.4%
HO-5	8.1%	5.5%	201-300T	6.9%	7.5%	501-1000	3.7%	7.9%	501-1000	7.1%	8.6%
HO-8	0.0%	0.1%	300T+	5.3%	5.1%	1000+	0.5%	1.6%	1000+	4.0%	43.4%
Wind Exclusion			Wind Prot. Credit			Replacement Cost			Ordinance/Law		
	Freq. Dist.			Freq. Dist.			Freq. Dist.			Freq. Dist.	
Type	1995	1998	Type	1995	1998	Type	1995	1998	Type	1995	1998
Yes	1.1%	1.1%	Yes	0.0%	0.0%	Yes	86.6%	93.0%	Yes	NA	92.1%
No	98.9%	98.9%	No	100.0%	100.0%	No	13.4%	7.1%	No	NA	7.9%
New York											
Policy Form			Policy Limits			Fire Deductibles			Wind Deductibles		
	Freq. Dist.			Freq. Dist.			Freq. Dist.			Freq. Dist.	
Type	1995	1998	Type	1995	1998	Type	1995	1998	Type	1995	1998
HO-1	0.3%	0.3%	≤100T	24.2%	18.0%	100-250	80.0%	70.0%	100-250	79.9%	68.1%
HO-2	19.0%	19.8%	101T-200T	54.9%	55.1%	251-500	15.7%	23.0%	251-500	15.7%	21.6%
HO-3	71.7%	72.8%	201T-300T	13.6%	18.3%	501-1000	3.8%	6.2%	501-1000	3.8%	5.7%
HO-5	9.0%	7.1%	301T-400T	3.8%	4.7%	1000+	0.6%	0.9%	1000+	0.7%	4.6%
HO-8	0.0%	0.0%	500T+	3.5%	3.9%						
Wind Exclusion			O-P Theft Exclusion			Replacement Cost			Ordinance/Law		
	Freq. Dist			Freq. Dist			Freq. Dist			Freq. Dist	
Type	1995	1998	Type	1995	1998	Type	1995	1998	Type	1995	1998
Yes	0.0%	0.0%	Yes	0.0%	7.3%	Yes	68.9%	67.7%	Yes	NA	65.8%
No	100.0%	100.0%	No	100.0%	92.7%	No	31.1%	32.3%	No	NA	34.3%

Source: ISO Data Base

In New York, in 1998, HO3 policies only represented about 72.8 percent of all policies, with HO2 policies accounting for 19.8 percent. HO5 policies constituted 7.1 percent of all policies in our database in 1998. As in Florida, we see a shift from HO5 policies to HO3 policies. Additionally, there was a slight increase in HO2 policies. We also see an increase in policy limits in New York between 1995 and 1998. Further, fire and wind deductibles increased in New York, but to a much lesser degree than in Florida. It is reasonable to surmise that New York's lower catastrophe risk lessens the need to increase deductibles. Changes in other policy provisions were also negligible in New York, although the proportions of policies with replacement cost on contents (67.7 percent) and additional ordinance/law coverage (65.8 percent) are significantly lower in New York than in Florida.[26]

[26] The demand for additional ordinance/law coverage may be greater in Florida due to upgrades in building codes to make homes more resistant to hurricanes.

4. MARKET CONDUCT AND PERFORMANCE

Analyzing insurers' conduct and performance in catastrophe insurance markets is difficult because of the low-probability, high-consequence (LPHC) nature of disasters and regulatory impediments to market adjustments. We can look at the level and structure of prices, but we must also consider differences in risk. Historical profitability, a standard performance measure, can be skewed by infrequent but severe catastrophes. In years when there are no major disasters, insurers may appear to be earning excessive profits, while one severe disaster can generate losses that consume the income earned over many years. The relationship between insurers' rates and expected losses, including a catastrophe component, is more meaningful but difficult to determine. Here we examine prices and several profitability measures from a more general perspective to set the context for our theoretical model and econometric analysis in Chapters 3-4.

4.1 Prices

There is great interest in the price of insurance but it is difficult to develop a summary measure that conveys all the information one would like. The premium charged for a specific insurance policy for a specific home can vary significantly due to a number of factors, including the expected insured loss that would result under the policy conditions specified. We look at changes in the average premium per insured home as well as the specific premium for a hypothetical home and policy. In our empirical work on demand in Chapter 4, we will examine a more refined measure of price.

Information on average homeowners premiums by state is available from the NAIC (2001a). Figure 2.3 compares the average premium per home in 1996 and 1999 in Florida, New York and countrywide for HO3 policies on homes with Coverage A limits between \$175,000-\$200,000.[27] We see from this figure that the average premium in Florida in 1999 - \$934 - was considerably greater than the average premium in New York - \$568 - and countrywide - \$567. The average premium also increased by a greater

[27] These data are only available for the period 1996-1999. If we were able to trace the increase in average premiums from the time of Hurricane Andrew to the present, we would have a greater appreciation of the impact of catastrophe risk on average premiums. We should note, however, that the increase in average premiums could be mitigated by insureds opting for larger deductibles and other options that would lessen premium increases. In fact, average premiums in the three jurisdictions actually fell from 1997 to 1998. Based on other price indicators discussed below, we believe this is due to changes in the amount of insurance purchased (e.g., selection of higher deductibles), rather than decreases in insurers' rates. We should also note that the Florida average premium is moderated by premium levels in low-risk areas in Florida.

percentage in Florida than in New York and countrywide, although even the Florida increase was relatively small. One reason for these disparities is the higher catastrophe risk in Florida. While Florida homeowners may be getting accustomed to their relatively higher rates, this likely increases the saliency of regulatory issues involving homeowners insurance and imposes political pressures on insurers and government officials (Meier, 1988).

Figure 2.3
Average Premiums
HO3: Policy Limit $175,000-$200,000

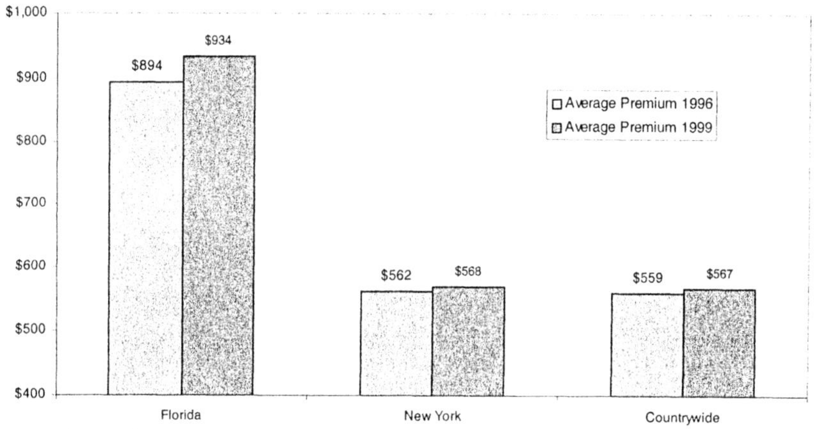

Source: NAIC

Of course, these are average statewide and countrywide premiums and reflect changes in the bundle of services that insureds purchase in a contract, as well as changes in insurers' rate structures. Another way to examine price trends is to track the premium that an insurer would charge for a hypothetical policy and home in different locations in a state. Figures 2.4(a)–2.4(b) present some information from ISO's Homeowners Premium Comparisons for Florida for 1992 and 1996 (the report was discontinued after 1996). In these figures, we compare the premiums four leading insurers would have charged for an HO3 policy for a frame home with a Coverage A limit of $150,000 and Protection Class 3 in Miami Beach (Figure 2.4(a)) and Orlando (Figure 2.4(b)).

Figure 2.4(a)
Florida Homeowners Premium Comparisons
Miami Beach: HO3, Frame, Protection Class 3, $150,000 Limit

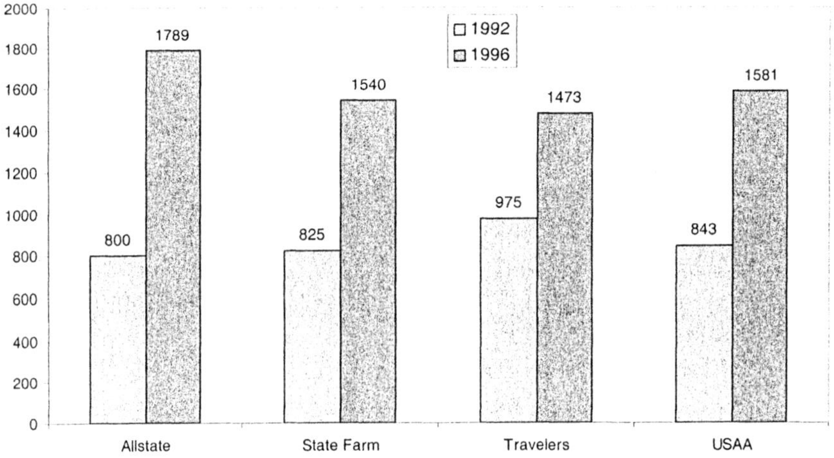

Source: ISO Premium Comparisons

Figure 2.4(b)
Florida Homeowners Premium Comparisons
Orlando: HO3, Frame, Protection Class 3, $150,000 Limit

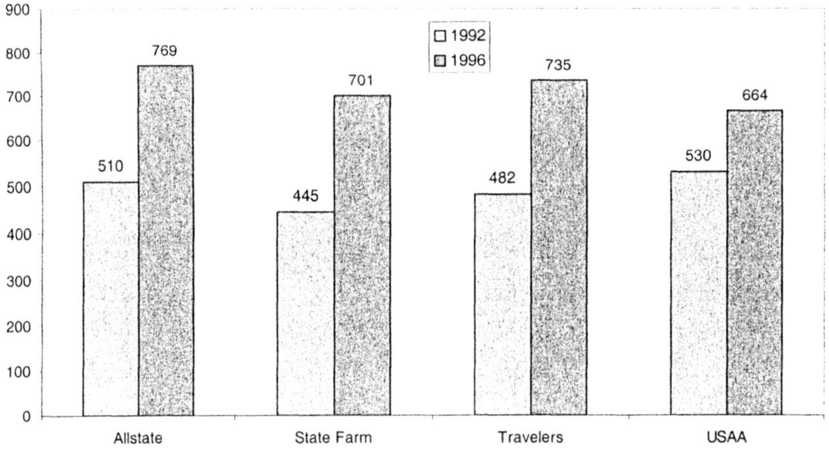

Source: ISO Premium Comparisons

We can see that all four insurers significantly increased their premiums in Miami Beach from 1992 to 1996 – the increase ranged from 51.1 percent to 123.6 percent among the four insurers. The hypothetical premiums also increased in Orlando, but to a much lesser degree than in Miami Beach. The insurers' Miami Beach premiums for 1996 are more than two times higher than their corresponding premiums for Orlando.

This suggests that both overall price levels in the state and price differentials between coastal and non-coastal areas increased significantly. This is consistent with what we would expect to see as insurers adjusted their rates to reflect increased catastrophe risk and other factors. That premiums in Miami Beach were higher than premiums in Orlando is consistent with the greater vulnerability of coastal areas to the brunt of hurricanes and tropical storms. It should be noted that regulators may have constrained insurers' rate increases and territorial differentials relative to what would have been actuarially indicated. It would be interesting to examine what happened to premiums after 1996 as regulators reportedly eased constraints.[28]

Figure 2.5(a)
New York Homeowners Premium Comparisons
Suffolk County: HO3, Frame, Protection Class 4, $150,000 Limit

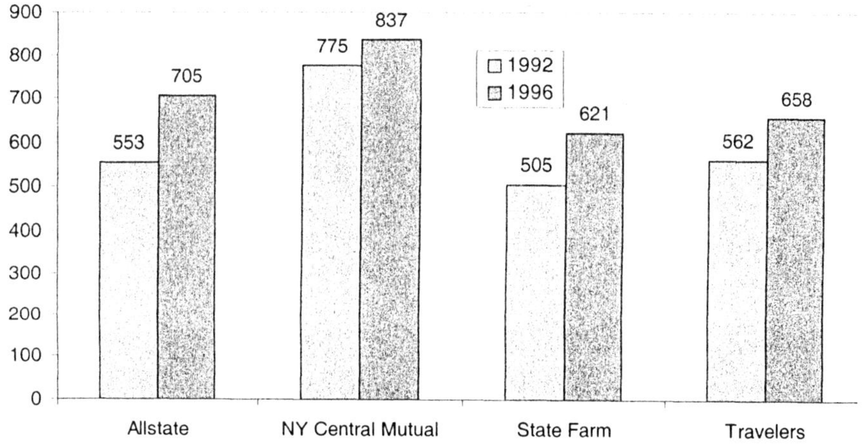

Source: ISO Premium Comparisons

We also present a similar premium comparison for New York in Figures 2.5(a)–2.5(b) to illustrate the difference between the two states. Between 1992 and 1996, all four selected insurers increased their premiums in Suffolk County on Long Island, with the increases ranging between 8 and 27.5 percent. In Albany, the insurers show various patterns: small increases, small decreases, or no change. Also, all four insurers charge higher premiums in Suffolk County than in Albany, but the difference between Albany and Suffolk County is much less than the difference between Miami Beach and Orlando. This pattern is consistent with what we would expect. Premiums increased moderately in Suffolk County where there is some catastrophe risk, but not as much as in Miami Beach, where catastrophe risk is much

[28] Data from the Florida Department of Insurance website suggest that rates continued to increase after 1996 and the difference between coastal and inland rates also widened.

greater. In Albany, where catastrophe risk is relatively minimal, there was very little change.

Figure 2.5(b)
New York Homeowners Premium Comparisons
Albany: HO3, Frame, Protection Class 3, $150,000 Limit

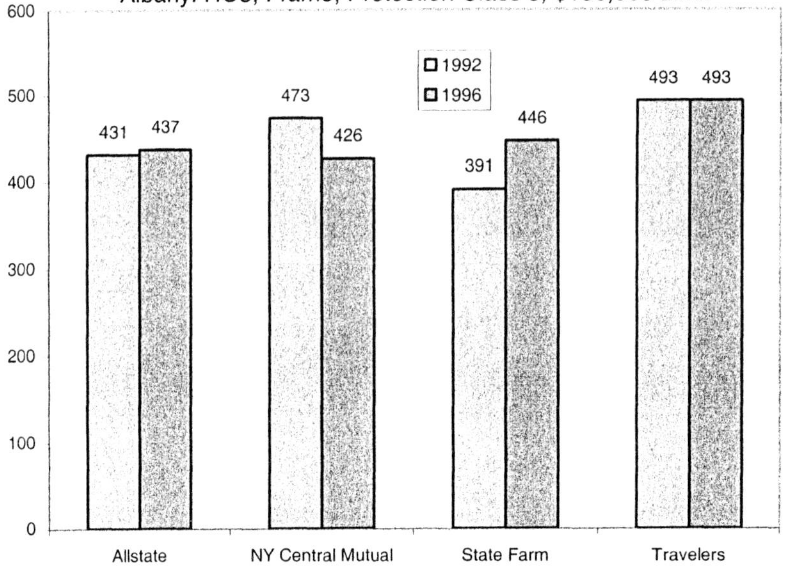

Source: ISO Premium Comparisons

4.2 Profitability

Three measures or indicators of profitability are examined at the state and countrywide levels: 1) loss ratios; 2) profits on insurance transactions; and 3) estimated rates of return on net worth. These data were obtained from NAIC (2001b). In addition, we can examine combined ratios and operating ratios at the countrywide level obtained from A.M. Best (2001). It should be noted that each of these profitability measures has its advantages and disadvantages in evaluating insurance market performance. Tables 2.5-2.7 summarize the results for Florida, New York and countrywide.

The loss ratio indicates the relationship of incurred losses to premiums earned, which is the principal but not the only factor affecting insurers' profitability in a particular line and state. Profit on insurance transactions, as calculated by the National Association of Insurance Commissioners (NAIC), reflects expenses, taxes and investment income, as well as losses, attributable to the underwriting of a particular line of insurance in a state. In this respect, it is a more inclusive measure than the loss ratio, but it also necessarily includes some formula-based allocations of certain financial items (that are not reported on a by line/by state basis). The rate of return on net worth, as calculated by the NAIC, includes investment income attributable to insurers' surplus, as well as profits on insurance transactions, and requires the formula-based allocation of surplus by line and state. These variables are calculated on a direct basis, before reinsurance, as data on a net (of reinsurance) basis are not available at the state level.

Additionally, we show combined and operating ratios published by A.M. Best at the countrywide level. The combined ratio reflects both losses and expenses in relation to premiums earned. The operating ratio reflects losses, expenses and investment income. These measures are calculated on a net (of reinsurance) basis.

It helps to keep in mind that, unlike profit on insurance transactions and rates of return on net worth, high loss ratios, combined ratios and operating ratios indicate low profitability. Loss ratios above 100 indicate that losses exceeded premiums. Combined ratios above 100 indicate losses and underwriting expenses exceeded premiums. Operating ratios above 100 indicate a loss on underwriting even after taking investment income into account.

Table 2.5
Profitability: Homeowners Multiperil
Florida: 1990-2000

Year	DPE (000s)	Losses (000s)	Loss Ratio	Profit	ROE
1990	973,036	577,010	59.3%	4.3%	13.3%
1991	1,040,068	666,684	64.1%	0.5%	6.9%
1992	1,109,897	10,991,310	990.3%	-657.4%	-714.9%
1993	1,223,902	1,231,245	100.6%	-19.9%	-16.1%
1994	1,543,654	592,763	38.4%	21.8%	35.4%
1995	1,595,646	933,453	58.5%	6.0%	13.1%
1996	1,851,407	694,278	37.5%	22.0%	33.6%
1997	2,160,796	732,510	33.9%	22.0%	31.5%
1998	2,285,064	758,641	33.2%	22.1%	29.3%
1999	2,543,780	845,979	33.3%	22.1%	28.6%
2000	2,838,645	902,770	31.8%	23.1%	31.3%
Avg.	1,742,354	1,720,604	134.6%	-48.5%	-46.2%

Source: NAIC

Table 2.6
Profitability: Homeowners Multiperil
New York: 1990-2000

Year	DPE (000s)	Losses (000s)	Loss Ratio	Profit	ROE
1990	1,501,551	813,841	54.2%	9.2%	20.2%
1991	1,580,650	995,810	63.0%	2.5%	9.6%
1992	1,651,640	1,080,173	65.4%	3.1%	11.2%
1993	1,719,035	985,007	57.3%	6.6%	14.5%
1994	1,808,119	1,386,827	76.7%	-7.5%	-5.6%
1995	1,907,520	965,205	50.6%	11.5%	19.7%
1996	1,999,463	1,235,668	61.8%	3.5%	9.4%
1997	2,071,286	938,293	45.3%	13.7%	19.6%
1998	2,149,080	1,076,689	50.1%	10.4%	15.4%
1999	2,203,618	1,123,845	51.0%	10.2%	14.6%
2000	2,292,719	1,074,210	46.9%	12.8%	18.2%
Avg.	1,898,607	1,061,415	56.6%	6.9%	13.3%

Source: NAIC

Table 2.7
Profitability: Homeowners Multiperil
Countrywide: 1990-2000

Year	DPE (000s)	Losses (000s)	Loss Ratio	Comb. Ratio*	Oper. Ratio*	Profit	ROE
1990	18,504,957	13,157,024	71.1%	113.0%	107.8%	-4.3%	-0.9%
1991	19,352,271	14,688,374	75.9%	117.7%	112.3%	-8.0%	-6.6%
1992	20,537,907	25,590,232	124.6%	158.4%	151.9%	-40.2%	-54.3%
1993	21,923,226	15,236,642	69.5%	113.6%	107.3%	-2.2%	2.5%
1994	23,600,467	16,921,535	71.7%	118.4%	113.5%	-4.4%	-1.7%
1995	24,944,550	16,762,738	67.2%	112.7%	107.4%	-1.2%	3.7%
1996	26,466,652	20,220,522	76.4%	121.7%	116.8%	-7.4%	-4.2%
1997	27,985,192	15,531,782	55.5%	101.0%	96.4%	5.4%	12.4%
1998	29,939,361	19,041,434	63.6%	109.4%	104.8%	-0.7%	5.4%
1999	31,564,464	20,106,564	63.7%	108.2%	103.8%	-0.1%	5.4%
2000	33,893,739	22,507,112	66.4%	111.4%	107.1%	-1.9%	3.8%
Avg.	25,337,526	18,160,360	73.9%	116.9%	111.7%	-5.9%	-3.1%

* From A.M. Best on net basis.

Source: NAIC and A.M. Best

4.3 Florida

Loss costs are the most important driver of insurers' overall profitability for most lines of insurance, including homeowners. Hence, analysts look closely at loss ratios as an indicator of rate or premium adequacy in a particular state and line.[29] Tables 2.5-2.7 track changes in loss ratios for the selected states and countrywide over the period 1990-2000. It is important to recognize that we are focusing on annual data in this analysis, which would be expected to be highly sensitive to catastrophes. One value of this exercise is demonstrating this sensitivity and the cash-flow management problem that catastrophes pose for insurers. Loss shocks to primary insurers that are not sufficiently moderated by risk diversification and liquidity mechanisms will have an impact on the supply of insurance.

For Florida, the loss ratio soared to 990.3 percent in 1992, reflecting the effect of Hurricane Andrew (Table 2.5). It is also abnormally high in 1993 at 100.6 percent, which probably still reflects adjustments for Andrew-related claims. For the period, the average Florida loss ratio is 134.6 percent, but only 43.3 percent when 1992 and 1993 are excluded. This indicates the volatility in loss experience in states with a high level of catastrophe risk and demonstrates the need to accumulate funds in years when catastrophe losses are low to cover claims in years when catastrophe losses are high, and/or employ some other catastrophe financing measures. Indeed, we should note that homeowners insurance losses in 1992, including those caused by Hurricane Andrew, were approximately nine times greater than the premiums earned in that year.

We also tracked total profits on insurance transactions (PIT) as a percentage of direct premiums earned and the estimated rate of return on net worth or equity (ROE). These data also are shown for 1990-2000. Once again, the year Hurricane Andrew hit South Florida (1992) stands out in all of the data. In Florida, both the PIT and ROE were negative in 1992 and 1993. Further, in terms of average annual profits for the decade, the severity of Andrew losses resulted in a –48.5 percent PIT and a –48.2 percent ROE for Florida. After 1993, the estimated ROE ranged between 28.6 percent and 35.4 percent (with the exception of the 13.1 percent for 1995, when Hurricane Opal occurred). These returns may seem high relative to rates of return in most other industries, but they reflect the need to cover long-term average costs including years with extreme catastrophe losses and, possibly, the risk premium required to write insurance in more volatile regions.[30] Also,

---

[29] The loss ratio is the "purest" indicator, as it does not include allocations of company-wide expenses and non-premium income. However, to interpret loss ratios one must have some benchmark in mind that implicitly involves assumptions about appropriate expense and profit loadings and associated investment income.

[30] Both the PIT and the estimated ROE can be misleading in that they are affected by earnings on investments and realized capital gains. In years when insurers are forced to sell assets and record large realized capital gains accumulated during preceding years, it can make them appear more profitable than they really are when viewed from a long-term rate of return perspective.

as these figures are on a direct basis, they reflect neither the cost of reinsurance nor losses recovered from reinsurers.

4.4 New York

In New York, loss ratios and estimated profits for homeowners insurance have been much more stable. During the decade, the lowest loss ratio was 45.3 percent and the highest loss ratio was 76.7 percent. The average loss ratio for the period was 56.6 percent. This suggests that, while there is still some volatility in New York experience, it is probably more manageable for insurers and premiums, over time, have been closer to being adequate to cover losses and other costs. At the same time, data for this period do not reflect the potential severity of storms that could strike the Northeast. Even in New York, there is a need to incorporate a catastrophe loading in rates to cover potentially severe losses when catastrophes strike.

In New York, homeowners profits also have been somewhat more volatile than profits in other lines.[31] For the decade, the average PIT was 6.9 percent and the estimated ROE was 13.3 percent. While the long-term average returns are probably a bit lower than insurers might prefer, profits in recent years have been higher. These data suggest that market conditions in New York are more sustainable for insurers than they are in many other states.

4.5 Countrywide

Hurricane Andrew also had a significant effect on the countrywide loss ratio, which rose to 124.6 percent in 1992 (Table 2.7).[32] Obviously, a more devastating hurricane would have a much greater effect on loss ratios in the affected state(s) and countrywide. In the last decade, the PIT was positive in only one year and the ROE was positive in only four years. For the entire period, the average PIT was –5.9 percent and the average ROE was –3.1 percent. A.M. Best figures on the countrywide combined ratio and operating ratio are consistent with the NAIC profitability estimates. Except for 1997 (when the operating ratio fell to 96.4 percent), both ratios have stayed above 100 percent. These conditions are clearly not sustainable and help to explain why some insurers have exited the market entirely or are at least pulling out

[31] The high relative volatility of profits in homeowners insurance is demonstrated in Grace, Klein and Kleindorfer (1998).

[32] States other than Florida also suffered some losses from Hurricane Andrew after it moved through Florida to other areas, but Florida suffered most of the financial losses that were incurred. Hurricane Iniki also struck in 1992, contributing to the increase in the countrywide loss ratio and the unprofitability of homeowners insurance.

of certain states. Catastrophe losses have contributed to these adverse results, but there are probably other contributors as well. It follows that prices must rise and/or costs must be reduced in states besides Florida if the market is to stabilize.

Chapter 3

REGULATORY INSTITUTIONS AND POLICIES

Because of intense economic and political pressures, state governments have intervened in catastrophe insurance markets in significant ways. Insurers and insurance markets are regulated primarily at the state level (Klein, 1998b). Hence, the laws and regulations governing homeowners insurance transactions are set by the individual state legislatures and insurance commissioners, with legal disputes generally adjudicated by state courts. Regulatory policies vary among states based on market conditions, differing regulatory philosophies and political factors. This is evident in the different responses of New York, Florida, and other states to catastrophe insurance problems.

Most public and industry attention is focused on price regulation, but it is important to note that several aspects of insurance transactions are regulated with significant implications for market structure and performance. These aspects include rates levels, rate structures, policy forms, marketing, underwriting, claims adjustment, and solvency. It also is necessary to consider how these areas of regulation interact. Both Florida and New York subject rates and policy forms to prior approval and have actively intervened in other elements of insurance transactions, although with different political pressures and philosophies. We begin this chapter with a review of the regulatory framework for home insurance markets, followed by a discussion of regulatory policies in various states and particularly in Florida and New York.

1. THE FRAMEWORK FOR INSURANCE REGULATION

Insurance regulatory functions can be divided into two primary categories: 1) solvency regulation; and 2) market regulation. Solvency regulation seeks to protect policyholders against the risk that insurers will not be able to meet their financial obligations. Market regulation attempts to ensure fair and reasonable insurance prices, products and trade practices. Solvency and market regulation are closely related and must be coordinated to achieve their specific objectives. Regulation of rates and market practices will affect insurers' financial performance, and solvency regulation constrains the prices and products that insurers can reasonably offer.

All U.S. insurers are licensed in at least one state and are subject to solvency and market regulation in their state of domicile and other states in which they are licensed to sell insurance. Reinsurers domiciled in the U.S. also are subject to the solvency regulation of their domiciliary state. Some U.S. and non-U.S. insurers write certain specialty and high-risk coverages on a non-admitted or surplus lines basis that is not subject to price and product regulation. Insurance commissioners still regulate entry to surplus lines markets by imposing minimum solvency and trust deposit requirements, approving consumer access to surplus lines insurers, and licensing intermediaries who are allowed to broker surplus lines transactions.

1.1 Solvency Regulation

Solvency regulation is intended to impose an upward bound on the level of insurers' insolvency risk in accordance with society's preference for safety. Regulators protect policyholders and society in general against excessive insurer insolvency risk by requiring insurers to meet certain financial standards and to act prudently in managing their affairs. State statutes require insurers to meet minimum capital and surplus standards and financial reporting requirements, as well as authorize regulators to examine insurers and take other actions to protect policyholders' interests. Solvency regulation polices various aspects of insurers' operations, including: 1) capitalization; 2) pricing and products; 3) investments; 4) reinsurance; 5) reserves; 6) asset-liability matching; 7) transactions with affiliates; and 8) management.

If an insurer fails to comply with regulatory requirements, or its financial condition becomes hazardous to policyholders' interests, regulators are authorized to intervene in various ways to control the insurer's activities. If an insurance company becomes severely impaired or insolvent, regulators will place it in receivership and either rehabilitate, sell or liquidate the company. State guaranty funds, financed by pro-rata assessments on the premiums of solvent insurers, cover most of the un-funded obligations of failed insurers to policyholders and claimants.

1.2 Market Regulation

Market regulation encompasses a diverse set of areas and is approached somewhat differently by the various states. Rates and policy forms are subject to some form of regulatory approval in virtually all states. State laws typically require that rates not be inadequate, excessive or unfairly discriminatory. For the personal property-liability lines, including residential property insurance, approximately one-half of the states require rates to receive prior approval before they go into effect (see Table 3.1). Other states allow insurers to implement personal lines rates without prior approval, placing greater reliance on competition to regulate prices. Nonetheless, where prior approval is not required, rates must still be filed. In "file and use" states, insurers file rates and are then free to use them if they are not rejected by state insurance regulators. In "use and file" states, insurers can implement new rates and then file them, with the regulators retaining the ability to reject rates afterwards.

Except for workers' compensation and medical malpractice, rate regulation for commercial property-liability lines tends to be less restrictive than rate regulation for personal property-liability lines, with fewer states requiring prior approval. Nevertheless, regulators typically retain authority to disapprove rates if they find that competition is not working.

Historically, many property-liability insurers adopted rates filed by an advisory organization, such as the Insurance Services Office (ISO), or filed deviations from advisory rates. Since the early 1990s, advisory organizations and the states have moved to a system in which advisory organizations file advisory prospective loss costs (developed and trended loss costs including allocated loss adjustment expense), as opposed to final rates that reflect expense and profit provisions as well as loss costs. Insurers are allowed to file either loss cost multipliers that convert advisory prospective loss costs to the final rates or final rates as they did before the advent of advisory loss costs. The intent of this system is to promote independence and competition among insurers by having each set its own provisions for underwriting expenses and profits.

Table 3.1
State Rate Filing Requirements Homeowners Multiperil: As of July 2002

State	Type of Rating Law
Alabama	Prior Approval
Alaska	Prior Approval
Arizona	Use and File
Kansas	File and Use
Kentucky	Flex Rating
Louisiana	Modified Prior Approval
Maine	File and Use
Maryland	Prior Approval
Massachusetts	File and Use
Michigan	File and Use
Minnesota	File and Use
Mississippi	Prior Approval
Missouri	Use and File
Montana	File and Use
Nebraska	Prior Approval
Nevada	Prior Approval
New Hampshire	File and Use
New Jersey	Prior Approval
New Mexico	Prior Approval
New York	File and Use
North Carolina	Prior Approval
North Dakota	Prior Approval
Ohio	Prior Approval
Oklahoma	File and Use
Oregon	File and Use
Pennsylvania	Prior Approval
Rhode Island	File and Use
South Carolina	Prior Approval
South Dakota	Prior Approval
Tennessee	Prior Approval
Texas	Flex Rating
Utah	Use and File
Vermont	Use and File
Virginia	File and Use
Washington	Prior Approval
West Virginia	Prior Approval
Wisconsin	Use and File
Wyoming	No File

Note: In some states, commissioner may impose prior approval if market is deemed "noncompetitive."

Source: NAIC

In addition, insurers must obtain approval for the products that they sell and, specifically, the policy forms that they use. Regulators seek to ensure that policy provisions are reasonable and fair and do not contain major gaps in coverage that might be misunderstood by consumers or that would be inconsistent with state compulsory insurance requirements.

Regulators also police insurers' and agents' sales and underwriting activities to ensure that they adhere to certain standards as well as police insurers' claim adjustment practices to assure that claims are handled according to the provisions of insurance contracts. The objective is to prevent abusive practices, e.g., misleading presentations on insurance coverage that take unfair advantage of consumers or the failure to pay legitimate claims on a timely basis., that take unfair advantage of consumers. Responding to consumer complaints and performing market conduct examinations are the primary ways in which insurance departments regulate market practices.

1.3 Other Functions

State insurance departments perform various other functions that are part of, or related, to their regulatory functions. The insurance commissioner is generally held accountable for the overall performance of insurance markets under his/her jurisdiction, and this leads to a number of activities designed to support market operations. Enhancing consumer information about insurers' prices, products and financial strength is a critical function, given the heavy reliance on competition to ensure good market performance. This is accomplished by publishing brochures on how to purchase insurance and insurer price comparisons for selected hypothetical policies and geographic areas. Other functions performed by insurance departments include agent licensing and education, adjuster licensing (in some states), anti-fraud enforcement, coordinating market assistance plans, emergency response to disasters, collecting premium taxes and providing public information. In addition, insurance commissioners frequently advise legislators on laws affecting public policy on insurance.

1.4 Regulatory Resources and Constraints

Insurance is a large and complex business, and state regulators face significant challenges in achieving their objectives. The importance of information (and, in some cases, the lack of it) to insurance markets affects their regulation. Regulators establish and implement rules governing insurance transactions based on imperfect knowledge of the nature of the risk transferred and its cost. At most, regulators can attempt to enforce general restrictions on market activity and to prevent flagrant abuses without creating significant market distortions inconsistent with public objectives.

This necessitates considerable reliance on market forces, even in jurisdictions with more intrusive regulatory restrictions.

The states also are challenged in coordinating their actions and reconciling their economic interests in the oversight of multi-state and multinational insurers. On average, 80 percent of the premiums in a state are written by insurers that are domiciled in other states (Klein, 1995). Consequently, a state will tend to rely on the domiciliary regulators of its non-domestic insurers (insurers not domiciled in the state) and focus its own efforts on the solvency of its domestic companies and the market activities of all insurers operating within its boundaries.[1]

Regulators are limited in their ability to influence the availability and price of insurance in response to consumers' needs and economic and political pressures. If regulators suppress rates below costs, insurers will be disinclined to write insurance policies voluntarily, which will diminish the availability of coverage. Regulatory restrictions on policy terminations may delay insurers' withdrawal from a market, but they also may discourage entry and decrease the supply of insurance in the long run. Policymakers may seek to justify market restrictions on the basis of equity considerations (e.g., equalizing rates between low and high-risk areas), but such efforts are likely to impair market efficiency by distorting sellers' and buyers' decisions. Enforcing cross subsidies through rate regulation is highly problematic in a private insurance market where insurers can avoid selling under-priced policies.

The ability of an individual state to ensure adequate insurance coverage of catastrophe perils and to allocate the cost of this coverage among different risks also is constrained by its jurisdictional boundaries. The division of the principal solvency and market regulation responsibilities between states can lead to externalities between states and potential inconsistencies between their policies. Some states with a high exposure to natural disasters may seek to externalize some of their costs or risk to other states, but competition and regulation in other jurisdictions check this behavior. States also are limited in their ability to pool or spread catastrophe risks within their boundaries. In a voluntary private market, low-risk insureds will seek to avoid paying subsidies for high-risk insureds.

---

[1] Domestic insurers are domiciled in the state. Non-domestic, or foreign, insurers are not domiciled in the state. Admitted insurers are licensed in the state. Non-admitted insurers are not licensed in the state. Alien insurers are domiciled in a foreign country.

2. KEY REGULATORY POLICIES AFFECTING CATASTROPHE INSURANCE

2.1 Entry and Exit

The states control the market entry of insurers primarily to limit insolvency risk and enforce their regulation of insurers' market practices. Capital requirements for licensing (even under risk-based capital) are relatively low, but other aspects of the processing of licensing applications can significantly slow entry.[2] Entry barriers that do not protect consumers unnecessarily impede competition and restrict the supply of insurance. At the same time, states with severe availability problems need to guard against a tendency to set their entry and solvency requirements too low, which could have adverse consequences for consumers in the long run. There is some evidence to suggest that new insurers have entered residential property insurance markets to help fill the gap left by insurers who are reducing their exposures. Florida regulators, for example, have facilitated entry by new insurers to help depopulate Florida's residual market.

In recent years, regulators also have attempted to restrict exit to some degree, particularly with respect to the personal lines and catastrophe risks. Exit encompasses insurers' efforts to shed some exposures as well as efforts to completely withdraw from one or more lines within a state. Regulators attempt to prevent insurers' withdrawal from a market to maintain the availability of insurance coverage, but these efforts could prove to be counterproductive in the long run if they discourage entry. Exit can be costly for an insurer to the extent that it will lose sunk investments in developing its distribution system, reputation, knowledge of the market, and relationship with policyholders. Indeed, the costs of full exit from a state by a multi-line, multi-state company discourage insurers from such exits and tend to make it a permanent decision. This gives regulators some leverage in seeking to keep insurers in a market, but there is a limit to regulators' power in this regard. At most, regulators can slow exits and increase their cost but not ultimately prevent them.[3]

---

2 State fixed minimum capital requirements for a multi-line property/casualty insurer range from $500,000 to $6 million, with a median level in the area of $2 million. These requirements are supplemented by risk-based capital (RBC) requirements that vary according to an insurer's premiums, liabilities, assets and allocation of business among different lines. However, RBC does not directly account for catastrophe risk and RBC requirements are binding for very few insurers (Klein, 1995).

3 Insurers serving multi-state commercial risks will have a higher cost of exit than insurers that can exit a state without adversely affecting their ability to cover risks also having operations in other states. This increases the economic rent that a state can extract before it

Many states impose some general restrictions on exits in the form of prior notice requirements on policy cancellations and non-renewals.[4] More specifically, regulatory responses to insurers' attempts to shed exposures after a catastrophe include imposing moratoriums on policy terminations, such as in Florida after Hurricane Andrew, and forcing an insurer to exit from all lines, not just lines chosen by the insurer.[5] Such moratoriums and exit conditions can discourage insurers from market entry and writing new business, because they limit insurers' flexibility to shed business if it becomes necessary to reduce their concentration of risk exposures. It is possible that exit restrictions could force an insurer into insolvency, but this has rarely occurred. In most cases, insurers, with the help of the courts, can exit before they become insolvent. Of course, this is less feasible in the event of a severe catastrophe, which can cause an immediate change in an insurer's financial condition. In extreme cases, insurers may respond to severe exit barriers by establishing a single-state company to insulate the rest of its business from losses within a state. Regulators may permit such arrangements to maintain the availability of coverage at relatively low rates, but the ultimate effect may to further concentrate risk within the state and increase its vulnerability to mega-catastrophes.[6]

Some regulators believe there is a need for regulatory restrictions on the speed of insurers' withdrawal or adjustment of their concentration of exposures. This presumes that some insurers "overreact" to perceived increased catastrophe risk and withdraw from a market "too quickly", resulting in an excessive degree of market instability. Even if regulatory exit restrictions can provide some stability to the market in the short run, in the long run, they can lead to increased market concentration and a decreased supply of coverage. Exit restrictions also can adversely affect the policy objective of limiting insurers' insolvency risk. Indeed, regulatory constraints

---

forces an insurer out of the state. For a theoretical analysis of the consequences of exit restrictions on solvency-constrained insurers, see Kleindorfer and Klein (2003).

4 The NAIC's *Property Insurance Declination, Termination and Disclosure Model Act* prohibits policy declinations or terminations based on the location of a residence unless there is business purpose for the decision which is not a mere pretext for unfair discrimination. The act also requires insurers to give reasons for declining to insure a property, and 30-day advance notice for non-renewals.

5 Florida extended the moratorium in 1996 to business that insurers placed on their books in anticipation of the moratorium being lifted.

6 These single-state insurers may be well capitalized and their holding companies may supplement the insurers' funds through reinsurance and capital infusions if it proves necessary. However, a holding company's legal obligation to bail out a subsidiary is questionable, and the formation of a single-state subsidiary is intended to limit the liability of the holding company and subsidies to high-risk states. This strategy is understandable when regulators constrain an insurer's attempts to raise prices and adjust its concentration of catastrophe exposures.

on entry and exit could interfere with the market's movement toward an optimal level of risk diversification among insurers. Ideally, as some insurers reduce their excessive concentration of exposures in high-risk areas, other insurers would see opportunities and enter to fill the gap. This process will not guarantee "affordable" rates but it should decrease the "risk premium" that insurers require to cover catastrophe perils. It also would reduce the industry's exposure to financial impairment caused by a severe disaster.

Consequently, in the long run, regulatory restrictions on the movement of insurers and their capital could have the perverse effect of decreasing availability and increasing prices and insolvency risk. If regulators place severe, long-term restrictions on exits, new insurers will be discouraged from entering the market (because of the fear of the high cost of exit if they need to withdraw). At the same time, insurers already present in the state may seek ways to gradually decrease their exposures (even if it is costly to do so) and may raise their rates to compensate for the level of risk they are forced to retain.

2.2 Financial Regulation

Areas related to solvency or financial regulation that are likely to have the greatest significance for conditions in catastrophe insurance markets include: capital requirements, investment restrictions, risk limitation, reserves, reinsurance, intervention against financially troubled insurers and guaranty funds. Financial regulation and the other areas of insurance regulation are closely tied. In general, more stringent solvency regulation forces insurers to offer less favorable terms (i.e., insurers will have to charge higher prices or reduce coverage) on insurance contracts. On the other hand, regulatory attempts to force insurers to offer more favorable terms (e.g., lower prices, more generous coverage, etc.) can have a negative effect on solvency. Consequently, solvency regulatory policy can affect catastrophe insurance market conditions, and regulation of catastrophe insurance markets can affect insurers' solvency. There is an inherent tension between the regulatory objectives of limiting insolvency risk and ensuring available and affordable coverage.[7]

[7] Regulators would generally agree that solvency is their first priority but the availability and affordability of insurance coverage also are important objectives and these objectives must be balanced consistent with market realities and societal preferences. For instance, regulators could virtually ensure that no insurer would ever fail by imposing very stringent capital requirements and other risk limitations. However, such a policy may decrease the supply of insurance and raise prices to socially unacceptable levels. In practice, regulators (and the marketplace) tolerate some degree of insolvency risk in return for a greater supply of insurance. Guaranty funds have been established to diversify this residual insolvency risk across all policyholders, but the "flat pricing" of insolvency guarantees can impose

This tension is exacerbated by the division of primary responsibilities in regulating a multi-state insurer's solvency and market practices between domiciliary and non-domiciliary states. Under "normal" market circumstances when coverage is readily available and premiums are relatively affordable, non-domiciliary states may tend to favor more stringent solvency regulation of a non-domestic insurer than the domiciliary state. This is because the domiciliary state has the most to gain from the growth of the company in terms of employment and tax revenues, while insolvency costs are distributed among all the states in which the company writes business (Klein, 1995).[8] However, when a state is suffering from severe availability problems and cost pressures, it may favor less stringent solvency regulation of its non-domestic insurers to increase the supply of insurance and relieve pressure on its market.

For instance, a high-risk state may prefer that other states ease catastrophe risk limitations on its non-domestic companies to avoid a significant number of policy terminations. While such a measure might increase the long-term insolvency risk of these insurers, the regulators in a high-risk state may give more weight to the short-term political gains from maintaining the availability of insurance coverage. If an insurer does become insolvent because of its excessive concentration of catastrophe exposures in high-risk states, the current guaranty fund system distributes the insolvency costs among all of the states in which the insurer does business in relationship to their claims liabilities in the various states. Hence, other states bear a portion of multi-state insurers' insolvency risk from catastrophes in high-risk states, but do not reap the corresponding short-term political benefits from maintaining the availability of coverage.[9] The potential difference in interests between states with respect to an insurer's catastrophe risk could lead to conflicts between the states in how they regulate the insurer.

---

cross subsidies, cause moral hazard, and encourage excessive risk taking by some insurers. Regulators could force a suboptimal solvency-supply solution inconsistent with social preferences.

8 Further, the cost of the insolvency is spread to all U.S. taxpayers as the guaranty fund payments are deductible under federal income taxes.

9 Guaranty fund costs to other states stemming from insolvencies caused by Hurricane Andrew were limited (less than 10 percent) because the insolvent insurers wrote most of their business in Florida. However, a more severe catastrophe that would cause larger multi-state insurers to fail would impose a higher proportion of guaranty funds costs on states other than where the catastrophe occurred.

2.2.1 Risk Limitation

The issue of risk limitation received increased attention from regulators after natural disasters in the early 1990s. The NAIC added an interrogatory question to the financial statements filed by property-liability insurers that requires an insurer to report and certify that it has calculated its probable maximum insurance loss (PML), how its PML was calculated, and what provisions it has taken to protect itself from excessive losses. After receiving this information, regulators may elect to undertake a more detailed analysis, or other actions, if they are concerned that an insurer has not demonstrated that it is properly managing its disaster risk. The effectiveness of this approach remains unknown. There is a question as to whether regulators in catastrophe-prone states are likely to address an insurer's high concentration of risk because of the implications for the availability of insurance, which is a more immediate political concern. Regulatory action to force an insurer to reduce its catastrophe exposure could have a negative effect on the availability of insurance in disaster-prone states. Such actions could compel insurers to terminate policies and decline applications in high-risk areas that would reduce the supply and availability of insurance in these areas. Rating agencies, such as A.M. Best and Standard & Poor's, also have begun to consider an insurer's catastrophe risk in their rating evaluations, which increases insurers' incentives to diminish this exposure.

2.2.2 Reinsurance

Regulatory requirements governing insurers' ability to claim credit for reinsurance could constrain the supply of catastrophe insurance. Regulators require reinsurers to meet certain criteria to be considered "authorized" and allow a ceding insurer to account for anticipated recoveries from these reinsurers as assets. Primary writers may still have some incentive to transfer catastrophe risk to unauthorized reinsurers (i.e., reinsurers who do not meet regulatory requirements to be authorized), but the inability to credit surplus for this reinsurance is a substantial disincentive for such transactions. Hence, regulation of reinsurance credit could have a substantial effect on primary insurers' capacity and ability to insure catastrophe-prone areas. This could hamper the emergence of new reinsurance capacity to help alleviate catastrophe insurance availability problems if regulators are reluctant to authorize new reinsurers. But, the desirability of easing state restrictions on reinsurers must be balanced against the risk of allowing participation by reinsurers who will ultimately fail to fulfill their obligations in the wake of a major catastrophe.

2.2.3 Regulatory Intervention and Guaranty Funds

Regulatory actions against failing insurers and the use of guaranty funds are an important component of solvency regulation. Natural disasters pose a serious threat to state guaranty funds. Guaranty funds can accommodate short-term capacity problems by boosting assessment limits and borrowing funds, but high insolvency costs from a large natural disaster could severely tax the capacity of a guaranty fund and the market supporting it.[10] The current system of pro-rata guaranty fund assessments is not sensitive to risk and, hence, encourages greater risk taking by insurers and policyholders (Cummins, 1988). Risk-sensitive assessments would encourage safer behavior but they also could further tighten the supply of catastrophe insurance. Still, this could be preferable to arbitrary limits on risk. There also may be some value in exploring arrangements that would allow state guaranty funds to pool capacity in certain instances (e.g., natural disasters) to provide additional liquidity and further diversify insolvency risk. Such arrangements would need to be structured to avoid perverse incentives and externalities among states in their regulatory policies towards high-risk insurers and markets (Klein, 1998a). Without such provisions, a state could be encouraged to allow or force insurers operating within its jurisdiction to assume an excessive level of insolvency risk, since the costs of insolvencies would be spread among all participating states.

2.3 Policy Forms and Coverage Requirements

In regulating insurers' policy provisions covering catastrophe risk, insurance commissioners must balance the objectives of promoting adequate coverage, availability of coverage, and affordable rates. Historically, regulators have tended to frown on policy provisions that would significantly restrict coverage because of their concern that insureds will retain an excessive exposure to risk, knowingly or unknowingly. Regulators have allowed insurers to introduce some modifications to coverage provisions, such as increasing deductibles, offering different deductibles and limits for catastrophe losses, implementing percentage deductibles, and offering wind exclusions, to encourage loss prevention and make it more economically

[10] The ten insolvencies affecting Florida caused by Hurricane Andrew (an event causing insured losses roughly one-fifth the potential amount for a mega-catastrophe) exceeded the Florida guaranty fund's assessment limits and forced it to borrow funds against future assessments to pay claims. Legislation allowed the guaranty fund to issue a bond through the authority of the City of Homestead and help pay off this bond through a temporary 2 percentage point increase in guaranty fund assessment. In 1997, the bond was fully paid. California and Tennessee have enacted similar enabling legislation.

feasible to offer catastrophe coverage. The public interest could be served by allowing such policies if it enabled policyholders to share more of the cost of small losses, but retain protection against catastrophic losses that would exhaust their assets. This would help to lower insurers' total losses from a disaster but still provide insurance protection for severe damage to individual properties.

2.4 Price Regulation

Regulation of catastrophe insurance rates is one of the most controversial issues facing policymakers and insurance commissioners in a significant number of states. If an insurance market is structurally competitive, rate regulation should be unnecessary, unless the objective is to enforce cross subsidies. Enforcing cross subsidies through price regulation is difficult to accomplish if the offer and purchase of insurance are voluntary and insurers can avoid selling insurance at inadequate rates. Insurers will be disinclined to offer coverage at prices below cost, and consumers will be more reluctant to buy coverage for which the price exceeds the actuarial cost. Regulatory efforts to suppress rates below costs will cause economic distortions and potentially threaten insurers' solvency if exit is restricted.

The states employ different regulatory systems for homeowners insurance, and some have reported that they have restricted catastrophe insurance rate increases. This information was derived from a 1995 NAIC survey of state insurance regulators and may be incomplete and outdated. Based on the survey, it is apparent that even states with competitive rating systems may impose restrictions on rate increases in particular circumstances. Six states along the eastern and gulf coasts, including Florida, Georgia, and North Carolina, reported restrictions on catastrophe insurance rates; four of these states have competitive rating systems. In addition, three western states, including Washington but not California, reported catastrophe insurance price restrictions, one of which has a competitive rating system. This demonstrates that a state's rate regulatory policy cannot be determined solely from its rating law.

It is important to distinguish restrictions on rate levels from restrictions on rate structures. Rate level pertains to the overall amount of premiums that insurers are allowed to charge for a given level of risk exposure. Rate structure pertains to the price differences that insurers charge between different classes of risk. Regulators may restrict one or the other or both. Restrictions that do not allow insurers to charge actuarially indicated rates to various risks reflect explicit or implicit attempts to grant cross subsidies to high-risk insureds.

Regardless of the reality governing homeowners' ability to afford cost-based premiums, regulators and legislators face strong political pressures to subsidize insurance rates in high-risk areas. Political support for subsidies may be fairly concentrated among residents in high-risk areas relative to countervailing political pressure against subsidies in low-risk areas.[11] Equity issues and political considerations aside, however, it is very difficult for regulators to enforce cross subsidies within a state as well as across states when insurance is sold by private firms (as opposed to a government-imposed monopoly insurer). Even with coverage mandates, individual private insurers can find a number of ways (e.g., not marketing to high-risk areas) to avoid writing risks at rates below cost. Efforts to enforce cross subsidies also encourage greater risk taking among consumers and, ultimately, greater economic losses.

Figure 3.1(a)

ISO Loss Cost Filings: Florida Homeowners

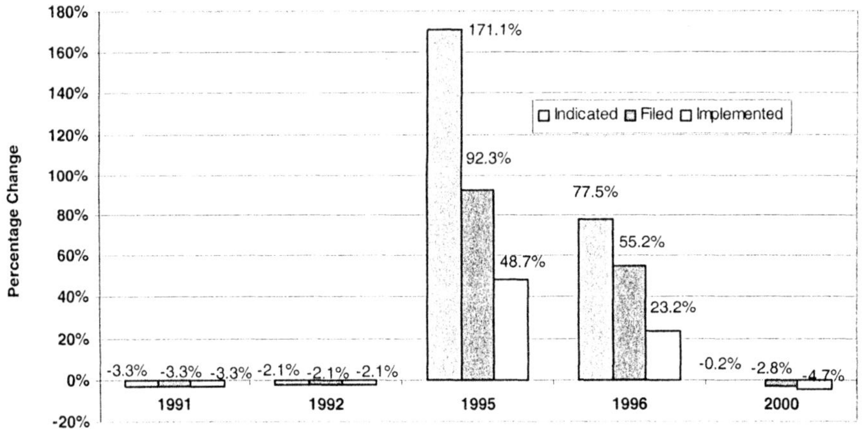

Source: Insurance Services Office

Discounting insurance prices for effective mitigation measures is another important issue. Insurers allege that inadequate regulatory ceilings on prices discourage them from implementing pricing discounts for loss prevention efforts by insureds. Their logic may be that any economic gains they would accrue from offering such discounts would be offset by greater losses from writing more business at inadequate rates. Research aimed at better catastrophe risk assessment as well as the effects of mitigation could help to solve both problems. If insurers and regulators can agree on adequate overall

[11] The economic theory of regulation suggests that concentrated economic interests will prevail over diffuse economic interests in influencing wealth transfers through regulation (See Peltzman, 1976).

rate levels and appropriate rate structures, insurers could offer price discounts that, at the margin, are equal to their expected cost savings from mitigation. This would increase homeowners' incentives to invest in mitigation and lower overall losses to the extent that it was cost effective to do so through mitigation. Ideally, homeowners should receive sufficient information to capitalize investments in mitigation over the expected life of their home. This should be reflected in the market value of a home when it is sold. The present value of even a small annual premium reduction could be significant if compounded over many years.

Figure 3.1(b)

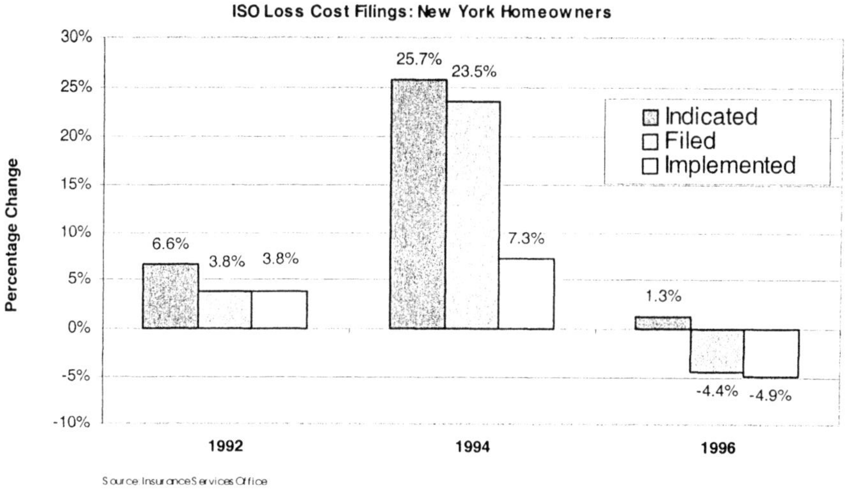

2.5 Underwriting Selection

Regulators have tended to impose very few restrictions on underwriting generally, but market reactions following disasters have generated more regulatory intervention in this area. As discussed above, regulators have focused more on restricting insurers' ability to terminate policies rather than forcing them to write new policies. Typically, regulators have restricted insurers' efforts to cancel blocks of risks based on their geographic locations. This is another aspect of the exit issue.

Several states reported that they placed restrictions on insurers' underwriting in relation to catastrophe insurance. Interestingly, the pattern here is somewhat different than that for price restrictions. Several states that did not report price restrictions did report underwriting restrictions. Northeastern states, Florida, Texas, and California, are among the states that reported underwriting restrictions. It is possible that some regulators view price and underwriting restrictions as a tradeoff and tend to emphasize one or the other. Price restrictions would be expected to prompt insurers to adopt tighter underwriting standards.

In addition, in areas subject to severe availability problems, legislators may be tempted to enact laws that restrict insurers' ability to refuse to accept new risks. For example, in 1996, the Florida legislature considered but did not enact legislation that would force an insurer to maintain a market share in coastal areas at least as high as its market share in other parts of the state. Such restrictions are difficult to enforce and counterproductive in the long run. Insurers' volume of business is affected by a number of different variables, including competition, many of which are not under the direct control of insurers or regulators. This type of regulation also would discourage the entry of new insurers.

2.6 Claims Adjustment

Regulation of insurers' claims adjustment practices following a disaster can have a significant effect on the cost and supply of insurance. Clearly, regulators must ensure that insurers meet the terms of their contracts. This becomes difficult, however, when contract terms are ambiguous with respect to certain circumstances, or claimants seek to retroactively expand coverage beyond that contemplated in their contract and the premiums paid. For example, there is the issue of whether insurers should pay the cost of rebuilding a structure to meet more stringent building code standards than those in effect when the structure was originally built. While homeowners policies generally include some ordinance or law coverage that defrays these costs up to a percentage of the coverage A limit, some regulators believe that all of the costs of complying with enhanced building codes should be covered under standard insurance contracts (without a special endorsement). Insurers and claimants also face a difficult situation when suppliers and contractors increase their prices after a disaster due to increases in the demand for their goods and services.

Although retroactive efforts to expand coverage may be intended to help claimants, it can subject insurers to unanticipated losses and encourage fraud and excessive risk taking. Regulators need to be careful in addressing claim disputes to maintain the integrity of policy provisions. The failure to do so could further discourage entry, lessen availability, and increase rates.

Regulators do have a substantial role to play in facilitating the claims adjustment process following a natural disaster. Regulators in California, Florida, South Carolina and Texas, among other states, have developed comprehensive disaster response programs that are key to recovery efforts. The NAIC has revised and expanded its disaster response manual based on the experiences of these states. This manual outlines a number of steps that regulators can take to expedite payment of claims from a natural disaster. These steps include providing an information clearinghouse for consumers and insurers and helping to support adjusters imported to deal with the flood of claims. Some states have even taken steps such as controlling the prices of building materials following a disaster. The economic implications of such policies on the supply of and demand for building materials and contractors' services could be problematic, however.

2.7 Residual Market Mechanisms

Residual market mechanisms (RMMs) are an important component of public policy towards catastrophe risk and insurance given the availability problems that arise. RMMs include assigned risk plans, windstorm and beach pools, joint underwriting associations (JUAs), and reinsurance pools. In theory, these mechanisms are intended to serve only as a secondary source of coverage for insurable risks that are unable to obtain coverage from the voluntary market. This assumes that RMMs charge adequate rates (i.e., do not run a deficit) and remain relatively small.

However, in reality, regulators sometimes suppress RMM rates below costs. This adversely affects the voluntary market in two ways. First, inadequate RMM rates discourage insureds from seeking voluntary market coverage if they can buy coverage through the RMM more cheaply. Secondly, the deficits incurred by RMMs because of inadequate rates are assessed back against insurers according to their voluntary market share. Hence, the greater the cross subsidy from the voluntary market to the RMM, the greater the tendency for the RMM to grow at the expense of the voluntary market which begins to accelerate into a "downward spiral". Also, with respect to catastrophes, insurers are exposed to risk not only through the policies they write voluntarily, but also through potential RMM assessments caused by a catastrophe. This further discourages insurer entry and encourages exit from the market.

The impact of RMM assessments caused by a catastrophe also affect guaranty funds, by increasing the financial hit to insurers and their potential for becoming insolvent. As noted above, the guaranty fund mechanism effectively redistributes insolvency costs to policyholders of all insurers, as well as taxpayers, in all of the states in which insolvent insurers do business.

FAIR plans were established in 27 states and the District of Columbia and Puerto Rico between 1968 and 1971. They were initiated in response to concerns about the availability of insurance in urban areas, but they have since been employed to address availability problems in some rural and coastal areas as well. FAIR plans typically offer fire and extended coverage for wind, hail, vehicles, explosion and smoke. Some states have expanded the policies they offer to include homeowners multi-peril and commercial property. Properties insured by FAIR plans must meet minimum underwriting or insurability standards established by regulators. A FAIR plan may operate as a syndicate, or through a single servicing carrier, or through multiple servicing carriers. Its rates are typically set by the insurance commissioner and any deficits are assessed against all insurers in relation to their voluntary market premiums for the relevant lines of insurance.

Additional insurance pooling arrangements in the forms of wind pools and beach plans have been set up in Alabama, Florida, Louisiana, Mississippi, North Carolina, South Carolina, and Texas to address catastrophe wind exposures. Insurer participation in these pools is mandatory. The plans in Florida, Mississippi, South Carolina, and Texas cover wind and hail only and are called windstorm plans.

A new concept of property RMM was established in Florida with the enactment of the Florida Residential Property Joint Underwriting Association in November 1993. The plan was extended to certain commercial property coverages (apartments and condos) in 1995.[12] The primary distinguishing feature of a JUA is that it is organized as a separate insurer rather than a pooling arrangement among a group of insurers. However, JUA deficits are assessed against all insurers, as are FAIR plan deficits.

Depending on how they are structured and regulated, RMMs can significantly exacerbate market problems. These mechanisms have the potential to mushroom and even supplant the voluntary market if their rates are out of balance, or other factors significantly restrict the supply of voluntary coverage. High assessments to fund residual market deficits can hasten insurers' exit from the voluntary market and discourage entry. Mitigation incentives can be undermined if residual markets rates are inadequate, or servicing carriers are not induced to control claim costs. RMM's cannot be used effectively to replace the voluntary market or substantially subsidize high-risk areas. At best, they can provide only a short-term safety valve for temporary decreases in the supply of insurance and a long-term source of coverage for a small number of high-risk properties.

2.8 Other State Government Risk Financing Schemes

The potential use of state-sponsored catastrophe risk financing mechanisms raises some interesting policy questions. The basic issue is whether the government (state or federal) needs to supplement private

---

[12] See Marlett and Eastman (1998) for a discussion of Florida's residual market arrangements for homeowners insurance and catastrophe risk.

insurance or reinsurance markets, and if so, what portion of the risk should the government underwrite. If the entry point for government insurance is set too low, it will unnecessarily "crowd out" private markets and introduce potential imperfections at a level that could be avoided by relying on private markets. On the other hand, if the entry point is set too high, there is a potential "capacity gap" between what private markets can insure and where the government program assumes risk. This leaves a layer of risk exposure that is not efficiently financed, with the attendant insolvency risks and costs described above.

There is significant debate about the appropriate entry point for government programs. This debate is complicated by the assessment of the "capacity gap" at a state or regional level versus a national level. Also, private insurance, reinsurance and financial markets continue to evolve and expand their capacity, so the appropriate entry point for government insurance/reinsurance is a moving target (see Lewis and Murdock, 1996).

California, Florida and Hawaii have established state catastrophe funds that have somewhat different structures.[13] Regulators generally believe that these mechanisms can be effective in providing an intermediate layer of excess reinsurance coverage, or supplementing the primary market in the case of Hawaii. Presumably, such mechanisms could promote greater economic efficiency if they facilitate more effective risk pooling within a state, or can utilize state government guarantees and recoupment mechanisms to facilitate long-term risk financing which facilitates the inter-temporal diversification of risk. Public insurers also may be able to secure favorable tax treatment for catastrophe reserves that may be denied to private insurers because of the government's difficulty in preventing private insurers from manipulating reserves for other purposes.

If state risk pools supplement (rather than supplant) private market capacity, they could increase the supply of insurance coverage. However, such mechanisms cannot be used to enforce cross subsidies within a state unless they are established as a monopoly and all property owners are coerced to buy insurance. Otherwise, private insurers would be forced to compete with subsidized state insurance, would avoid selling and property owners would be disinclined to buy insurance coverage that was overpriced to support subsidies for high-risk areas.

State catastrophe pools are subject to geographic constraints that limit their capacity to provide a total solution to catastrophe insurance availability problems in high-risk states. A state mechanism can only pool exposures within a state. This insufficiently diversifies the risk of very large catastrophes within a state. States can accumulate tax-favored reserves over

[13] See Roth (1998) and Lecomte and Gahagan (1998) for a detailed discussion of the California and the Florida funds, respectively.

time, as well as borrow money if necessary, but the size of their markets still limits the amount of funds they can accumulate or borrow. Rough estimates of the total catastrophe capacity (including state pools) for Florida or California are $10-$12 billion. This falls considerably short of the potential $50-$80 billion in insured losses that could occur from a severe catastrophe in a major population center of either state.

Consequently, state regulators believe that additional capacity is needed beyond that which can be provided by single-state pools. Several states have called for federal legislation to establish a mechanism to provide this additional capacity. However, Congress is reluctant to expose the Treasury to a large potential liability. With the exception of federal insurance programs for flood, crops, and terrorism, national legislation to establish federal catastrophes insurance programs continues to be debated.

There is an important issue with respect to the financial soundness and market impact of the network of state catastrophe risk funding mechanisms, which include RMMs, cat funds, and guaranty funds. Insured losses stemming from a mega-catastrophe could overwhelm these mechanisms and cause rippling effects throughout the industry, which could harm a number of insurers and their policyholders, even in low-risk states. The interactions between these mechanisms and their implications need to be studied further to assess their effects on the viability of private insurance markets and insurers' attempts to manage their risk exposure.

2.9 Catastrophe Modeling and Regulation

One of the key innovations affecting markets for catastrophe insurance has been the development of credible models to predict the probability distribution of catastrophe losses for a given portfolio of insured properties. Companies such as AIR Worldwide, EQE and RMS, and some reinsurance brokers and public agencies, have developed models that provide a probabilistic assessment of the losses likely to be incurred by an insurer for a specific portfolio as a result of natural hazards such as hurricanes and earthquakes. Over the years, these "cat models" have increased in sophistication and in the completeness of the data they use, and they have become an important element in allowing both insurers and reinsurers to improve the management of their exposures and pricing of their products.[14] We will have more to say about the details of these cat models in the next chapter when we consider their use in pricing insurance products to cover

---

[14] For a more detailed description of catastrophe modeling and its uses in support of insurer and reinsurer decisions, the reader should consult Kunreuther et al. (2003), on which this section is based.

natural hazards. Here we wish only to point briefly to the growing importance of cat models in support of regulation.

Regulatory agencies have had to develop an understanding of catastrophe models as insurers increasingly integrate these tools into their day-to-day operations. Models provide a scientifically rational approach for quantifying an insurer's risk. By requiring insurers to report modeled loss estimates, the regulator can assess whether the company has been responsible in controlling their accumulations and in managing their exposures. Rates can be based on an integration of all possible events, not just a limited historical record. However, regulators may view a cat model with the suspicion that it is merely a tool to justify higher rates and to take away discretionary authority from the regulator. Given this tension, the development and acceptance of cat models for regulatory use has not been without controversy.

Added to the above tension is the fact that catastrophe models are complex products that require specialized expertise to evaluate thoroughly and, for competitive reasons, modeling firms usually are reluctant to provide detailed descriptions of their product's technical underpinnings. Differences in model assumptions can cause predicted loss results to vary considerably between modeling firms. Each may be reasonable within the data constraints and modeling assumptions about the hazard in question, but the range of uncertainty in catastrophe models can be disconcerting when compared to the actuarial precision available in lines such as life or auto.

As the states most at risk from earthquakes and hurricanes, California and Florida have been in the forefront with respect to the use of cat models in support of insurance ratemaking and regulation. For example, modeled results have been extremely important in setting up and capitalizing the California Earthquake Authority. The state of Florida has developed a review process by which modeling firms must show that their products meet a set of technical criteria. Insurers submitting modeled rates must do so using an approved model. In both states, the issue of modeling as a basis for rates has become politicized and has been subject to criticism by public interest advocates, who characterize such models as simply exercises in driving rates to unreasonable levels.

Other states have followed their own path. For example, Texas originally disallowed any rates filed on the basis of computer models, but later moderated this somewhat to allow rate filings to use model-based information as supporting information (see Mah, 2000). There have also been publicly developed models. For example, the California Division of Mines and Geology (CDMG) has begun to explore the process of calculating earthquake insurance loss costs with publicly-available models (Cao et al., 1999). These results then become a baseline for comparison with results from private firms. At the federal level, the Federal Emergency Management Agency (FEMA) has spent considerable effort over the past few years to develop the HAZUS loss estimation program. Initially developed for seismic risk, it is being expanded to cover the perils of flood and hurricane to provide the capability for "all-hazards" assessments. (FEMA, 2001). As an example of its impact, the Department of Geological and Mineral Industries (DOGAMI), Oregon's state geological survey, has used HAZUS extensively to quantify losses due to earthquakes on both a local and statewide scale (Vinson and Miller, 2000).

We return to the subject of cat models below in discussing our analysis of pricing of homeowners policies covering extreme events from natural hazards. While one might expect pricing decisions by insurers to be informed by disciplined quantification procedures involving cat models, the above comments also point out the critical importance that such models are beginning to have in the regulatory arena. Although there are significant technical and data differences between cat models, giving rise to real problems in using these models as rigid guides for solvency and ratemaking regulations, they are nonetheless becoming increasingly important in providing a discipline and a coherent logic for insurers in controlling their exposures and in supporting their arguments for rate adequacy and precision to regulators.

3. REGULATION IN FLORIDA

Post-Andrew market developments prompted the Florida legislature and insurance commissioner to impose the most binding constraints on insurers in any state (Lecomte and Gahagan, 1998). Florida restricted insurers' attempts to raise rates and reduce their exposures. Pricing constraints have taken two forms. One is a ceiling on the overall rate level that insurers can charge.[15] The second is a constraint on insurers' rate structures, i.e., territorial rating factors or differences in rates across various geographic areas of the state. This latter constraint is significant because the expected loss for a given property can vary widely depending on its proximity to the coast (where the force of hurricanes is most severe) and other features of the surrounding terrain. Regulators have compressed rate differentials between high and low risk areas in attempt to keep rates in high-risk areas more

[15] This kind of constraint is typically implemented through regulatory disapproval of the overall rate level increases filed by insurers. For example, an insurer may file for a 10 percent rate level increase, but regulators will only approve a 5 percent increase. To meet this constraint, an insurer must adjust its rating structure, i.e., all of its rates proportionately weighted by exposures, to produce the approved rate level change.

affordable. Note that rate compression is often associated with rate suppression. When regulators cap rates in the highest-cost territories, there is generally no compensating increase in the rates for low-cost territories. Consequently, this rate capping results in an overall rate level that is inadequate to cover the total cost of risk.

Insurers have been permitted to increase their rates gradually, however. Whether rates have reached actuarially indicated levels in all areas of the state is questionable. It does appear that there was considerable rate suppression and compression for most of the decade, and rates in high-risk areas were more constrained than in lower-risk areas (Muslin, 1996). Thus, it is useful to review these policies and contemplate their effects on market behavior during the period we study as well as in the future.

Figure 3.1(a) summarizes the disposition of ISO advisory loss cost filings with Florida regulators for the period 1991-2000. Prior to Hurricane Andrew, ISO filed for a 3.3 percent decrease in 1991 and a 2.1 percent decrease in 1992. Both changes were approved as filed. In contrast, in 1995, ISO filed for a 92.3 percent increase. However, the insurance department approved only a 48.7 percent increase. While this was a substantial increase, it was inadequate relative to actuarial indications based on models that incorporated catastrophe loss estimates. ISO followed with filing a 77.5 percent increase in 1996, but the insurance department approved only a 23.2 percent increase. In 2000, ISO filed a 2.8 percent decrease, but the department imposed a 4.7 percent decrease. This suggests that regulators suppressed rate levels generally for both insurers that utilized the ISO loss costs in their rate filings as well as insurers that made independent rate filings.[16]

While the trend in ISO filings suggests that overall advisory lost costs may have reached a level "within the realm of adequacy," it appears that some rate compression by regulators persists. Figures 3.2(a)–3.2(c) illustrate how insurers' rate structures have been compressed in Florida. These figures show indicated, filed and implemented (i.e., approved) base territorial loss costs, with territories ranked by the amount of the indicated loss cost. It is apparent from these figures that the disparity between the indicated and approved loss cost is much higher in absolute and relative terms for territories where indicated loss costs were higher because of greater catastrophe exposure and other factors. In 1992, this disparity was small and confined to only a handful of the highest cost territories. In 1996, the disparity was very large and existed for most territories, with the highest-cost territories subject to the highest relative (and absolute) disparities. In 2000, the disparities diminished but remained significant for the eight

[16] This supported by other analyses of the regulatory disposition of insurer rate filings (Muslin, 1996).

highest-cost territories. It is not coincidental that the higher cost territories tend to be located on the southeast coast of Florida.

Figure 3.2(a)

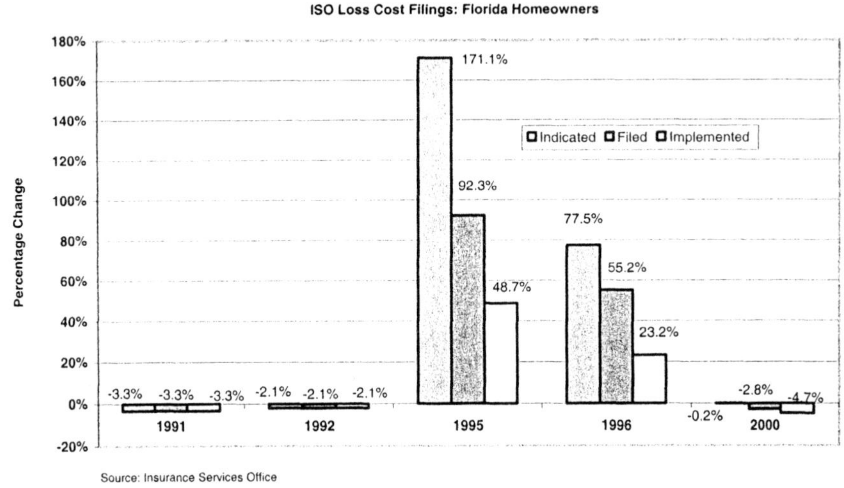

Figure 3.2(b)

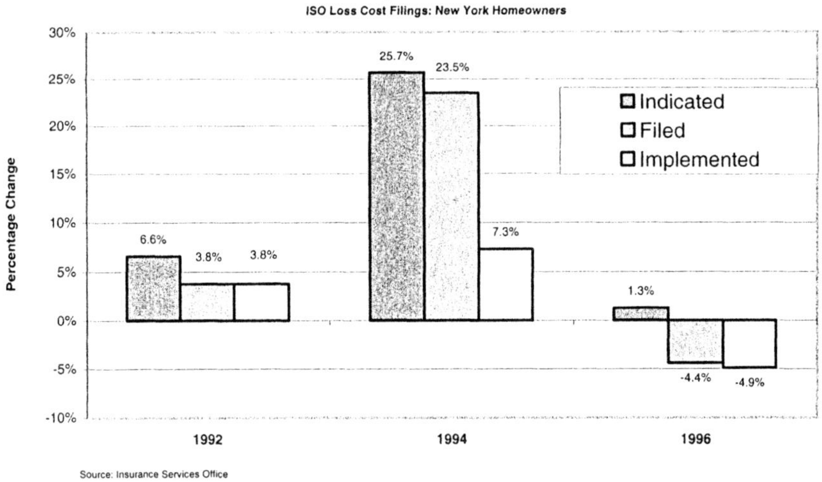

Ironically but not surprisingly, rating constraints conflicted with Florida officials' attempts to preserve the availability of coverage. After Hurricane Andrew, the Florida legislature enacted a moratorium on policy cancellations and non-renewals, which sunset on June 1, 2001. Hence, unless insurers negotiated a special exemption with the insurance department, they were only allowed to shed exposures through cancellations and non-renewals instigated by insureds. As a result, it is likely that many insurers were forced to retain a higher number of exposures in high-risk areas than they would choose to in the absence of regulatory constraints. This prompted concerns that policy terminations would increase and the residual market would grow with the end of the moratorium, and this is what has happened.

Figure 3.3(a)

Florida Homeowners Loss Costs: Indicated vs. Filed vs. Implemented: 1992

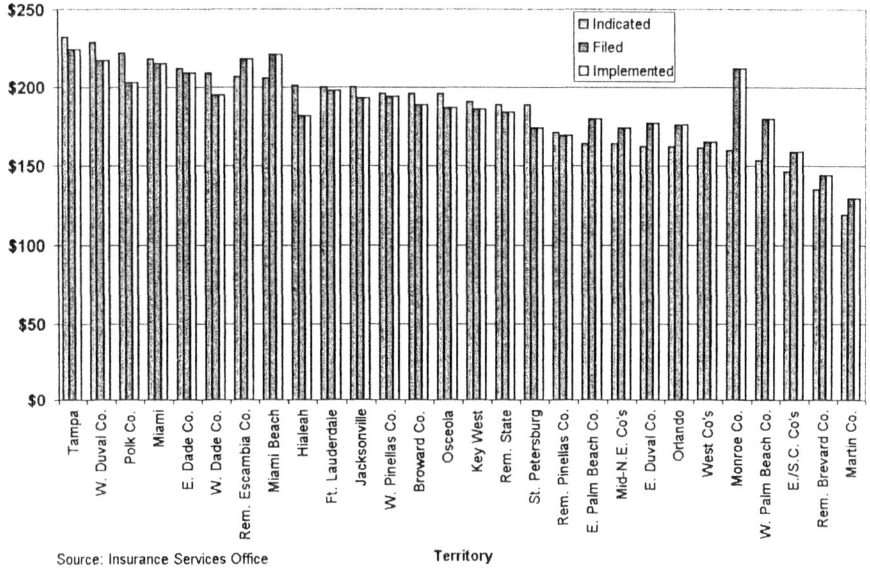

Source: Insurance Services Office

Figure 3.3(b)

Florida Homeowners Loss Costs: Indicated vs. Filed vs. Implemented: 1996

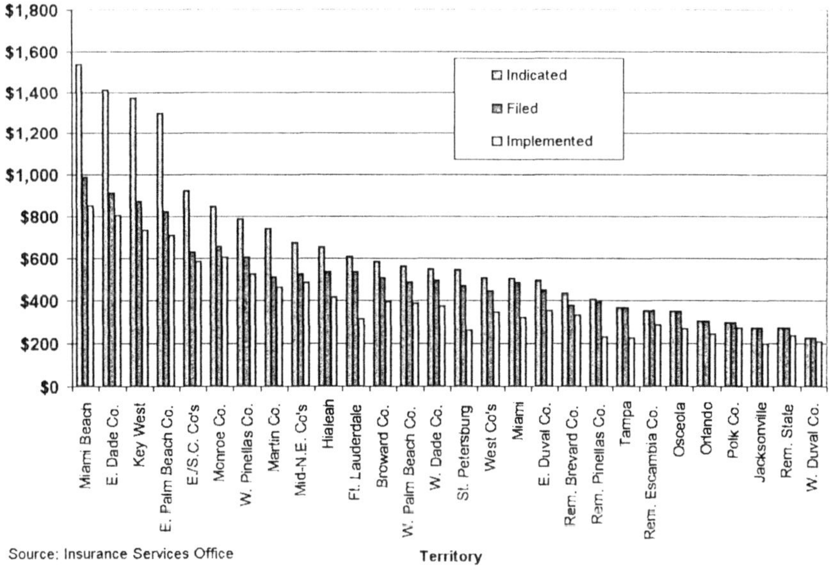

Source: Insurance Services Office

Figure 3.3(c)

Florida Homeowners Loss Costs: Indicated vs. Filed vs. Implemented: 2000

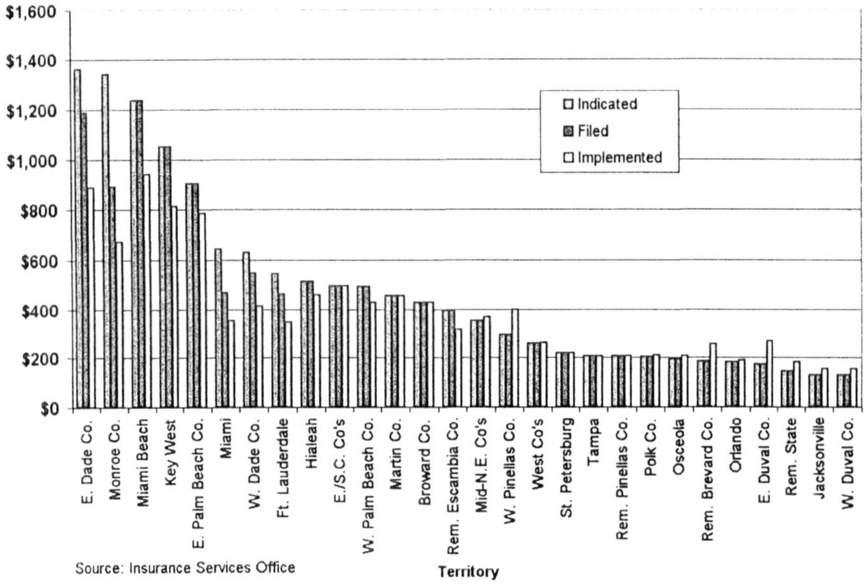

Source: Insurance Services Office

Nonetheless, some homeowners must still find coverage if they purchase a home or have to cancel or non-renew their existing policy for other reasons. If they cannot secure coverage in the voluntary market, they must obtain coverage through the state's residual market facility. This caused Florida's two residual market mechanisms (the JUA and the wind pool) to swell and complicate the management and financing of catastrophe risk.[17] The Florida Residential Property and Casualty Joint Underwriting Association (FRPCJUA) provided coverage for homeowners unable to obtain coverage in the voluntary market. It grew to 930,000 policies (approximately 30 percent of all policies in the state) after Hurricane Andrew. In August 2002, the wind pool and the FRPCJUA were combined into a new entity, the Citizens Property Insurance Corporation (CPIC). The facility imposes risk on all insurers and their policyholders, as any deficit it incurs is assessed proportionately against insurers based on their voluntary market shares. This has a detrimental effect on insurers' willingness to write policies in the voluntary market and forces them to retain some additional risk beyond their own exposures.

[17] See Marlett and Eastman (1998) and Muslin (1996) for a discussion of issues raised by public catastrophe risk financing mechanisms in Florida.

Figure 3.4(a)

New York Homeowners Loss Costs: Indicated vs. Filed vs. Implemented: 1992

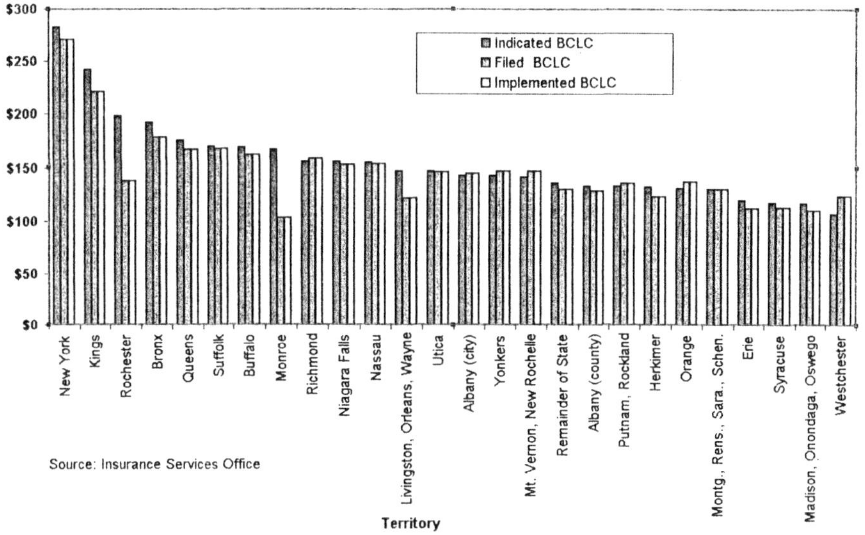

Figure 3.4(b)

New York Homeowners Loss Costs: Indicated vs. Filed vs. Implemented: 1994

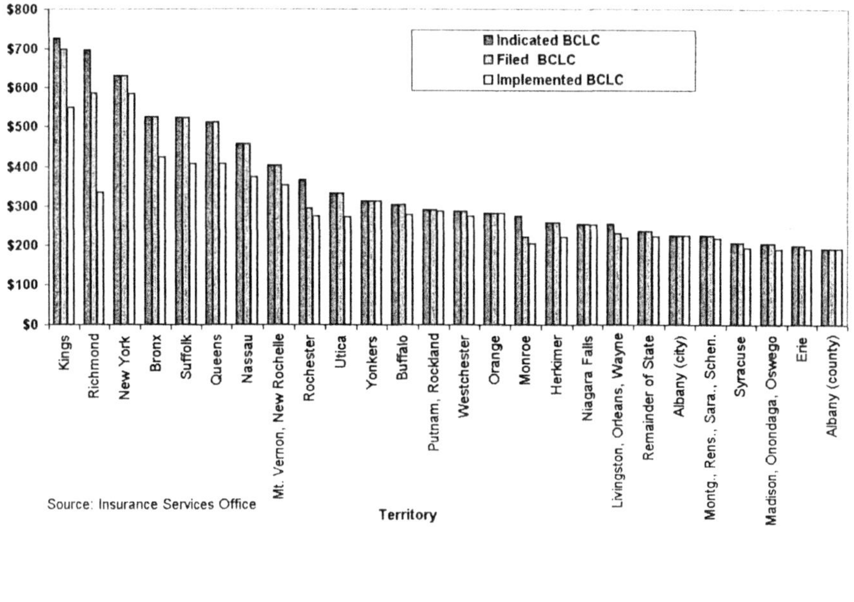

Figure 3.4(c)

New York Homeowners Loss Costs: Indicated vs. Filed vs. Implemented: 1996

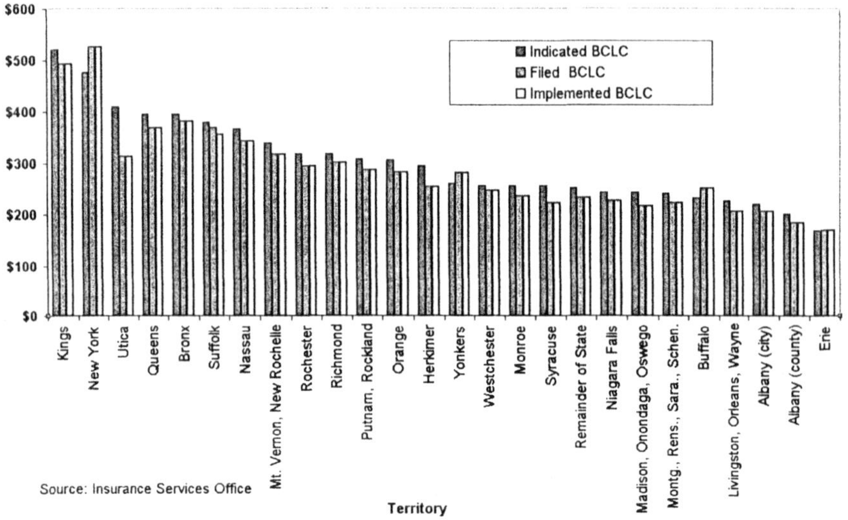

An aggressive depopulation program had reduced the JUA to a shadow of its former self (see Figure 3.4(a)). As of mid-year 2001, it only had 70,600 policies. However, this improvement has since reversed. When insurers took policies out of the JUA, they committed to continuing coverage for only three years, raising the prospect of some of those policies returning to the JUA. Indeed, policy counts (now full-coverage policies in the CPIC) rose to over 206,000 by December 2002. Understandably, these policies are heavily concentrated in Broward, Dade, Monroe, and Palm Beach counties where hurricane exposure is the greatest. Indeed, the total exposures on CPIC full-coverage policies has soared to $35.1 billion, indicating that the homes that have recently come into the CPIC are higher value dwellings.

Figure 3.5 (a)

Florida Residential Property JUA

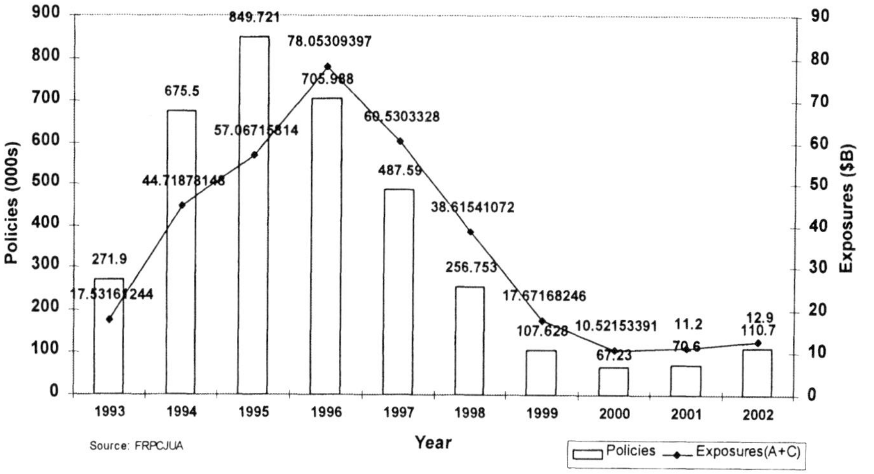

Figure 3.5(b)

New York FAIR Plan

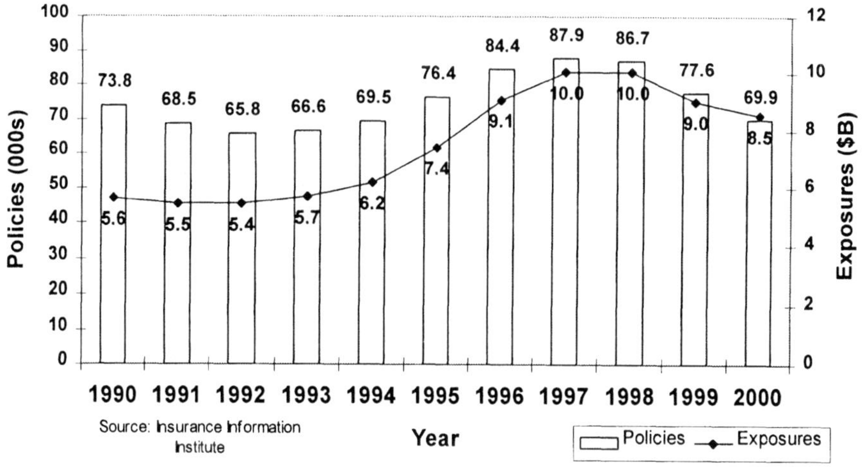

A second mechanism, the Florida Windstorm Underwriting Association (FWUA), had assumed the wind risk for many homes in coastal areas of Florida. Its policies now comprise the high-risk component of CPIC. For these policies, the CPIC provides protection against windstorms that compliments the coverage providing protection against losses due to other perils written by private insurers. Participating insurers share in the results of the experience on these policies and any deficits are assessed against the voluntary market.

Unlike the JUA, the FWUA continued to grow till 1998, as shown in Figure 3.5. It peaked at more than 500,000 policies and $91.1 billion in exposures at the end of 1998. It declined marginally to 398,222 policies by the end of January 2003, although exposures were even higher at $108.5 billion. While this mechanism has made it easier for insurers to continue coverage for non-wind perils, its financial structure presents problems. The CPIC's revenues and funds would not be sufficient to cover losses from a severe hurricane. Hence, its financial structure, coupled with its size, is a matter of concern. Most importantly, it means that a significant portion of catastrophe risk is still insured through a state-sponsored mechanism.

Figure 3.6

Florida Windstorm Underwriting Association

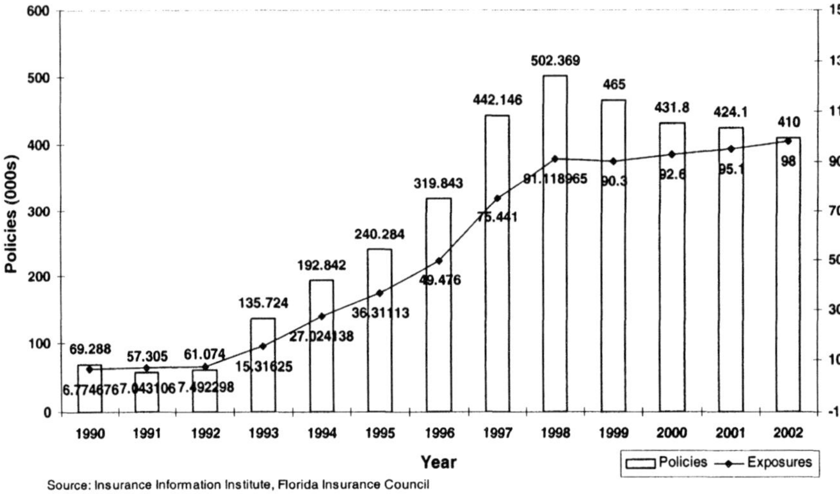

Source: Insurance Information Institute, Florida Insurance Council

Florida's catastrophe reinsurance facility and insolvency guaranty association pose some additional risk for insurers, insureds and the public, despite being intended to reduce risk. In 1993, Florida established the Florida Hurricane Catastrophe Fund (FHCF) to allow insurers to transfer a portion of their catastrophe risk in Florida (see Lecomte and Gahagan, 1998). The Fund's financial structure (as of June 2000) is depicted in Figure 3.6. The Fund will reimburse a portion of insurers' losses from a severe hurricane. It is funded by premiums paid by insurers that write policies on personal and commercial residential properties based on the insurers' property exposures. An important provision limits the Fund's obligation to pay losses to the sum of its assets and borrowing capacity.

Figure 3.7
Florida Hurricane Catastrophe Fund

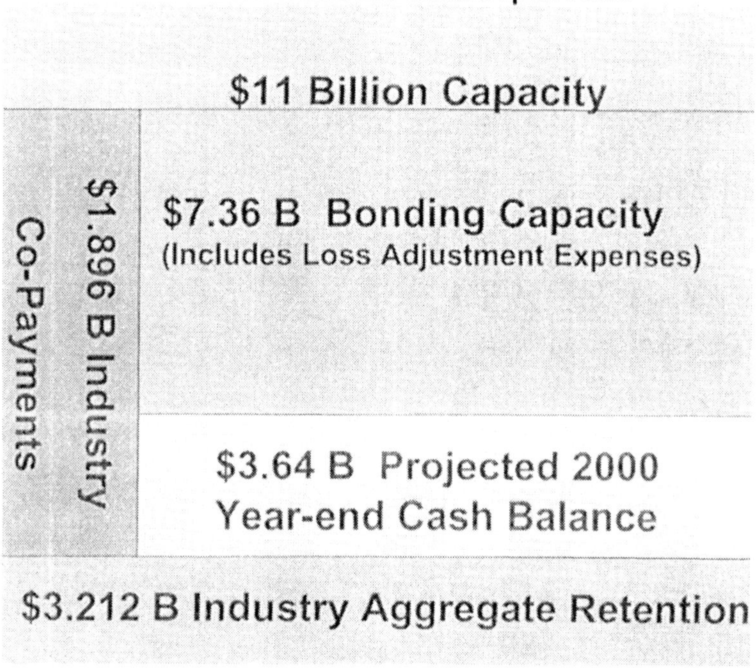

Source: FHCF Presentation, June 26, 2000

As of June 2000, the Fund was estimated to have a total capacity of $11 billion - $3.6 billion in cash and $7.4 billion in borrowing capacity.[18] Borrowed funds would be raised through the issuance of bonds to be repaid through a 4 percent assessment on all property-casualty insurance premiums in the state, excluding workers compensation. If the Fund lacks sufficient funds to pay all losses from a hurricane, each insurer will be reimbursed on a pro-rata basis from the funds available according to its share of the premiums paid into the fund for that contract year. Hence, the potential for special assessments as well as partial reimbursement for catastrophe losses imposes residual risk on insurers. Still, the Fund does provide some reinsurance protection that may have been unavailable immediately following Hurricane Andrew. Further, unlike private insurers and reinsurers, it can accumulate catastrophe reserves on a tax-exempt basis.

---

18 In the Fund scheme, the industry has an aggregate retention of $3.2 billion and potential co-payment obligations of $1.9 billion.

Like other states, Florida also has an insolvency guaranty association that is intended to cover the claims obligations of insolvent insurers. The guaranty association is important because it could experience severe stress if a large number of insurers became insolvent because of a catastrophe. The guaranty association's funding capacity is supported by assessments on property-casualty insurance premiums in the state that are limited to 2 percent annually. Hurricane Andrew directly caused nine insolvencies in Florida and the resulting demands on the guaranty fund exceeded its capacity. The guaranty association was forced to fully exercise its 2 percent assessment authority and the legislature authorized it to assess an additional 2 percent to repay funds borrowed to cover its capacity shortfall. The association eventually paid off its debts in 1997. Interestingly, the association's assessments caused a tenth insurer to become insolvent. The experience from Hurricane Andrew reflects the guaranty association's vulnerability to catastrophes and the potential pass-through of insolvent insurers' obligations and risk to other insurers. Hence, insurers with significant premium writings in the state, even in lower risk areas and lines of business, retain a secondary exposure to catastrophe losses through their potential obligations to the guaranty fund.

4. REGULATION IN NEW YORK

Pressures on residential insurance markets also prompted a governmental response in New York, but this response appears to have been less restrictive than in Florida. From the onset of market problems in 1992, New York regulators have worked with insurers in facilitating gradual adjustments in their rates and concentration of exposures. A full explanation of the reasons for New York's less restrictive approach is beyond the scope of this monograph, but two factors are evident. First, the severity of catastrophe risk and resulting market pressures have not been as great in New York as in Florida. Second, the New York insurance department has a history of working cooperatively with insurers to address market problems, reflecting a regulatory philosophy that may not be fully shared by all insurance departments.[19]

Figure 3.1(b) shows the regulatory disposition of ISO loss cost filings in New York. ISO filed for a 3.8 percent increase in 1992, which was approved by regulators. In 1994, ISO filed for a 23.5 percent increase, reflecting the its reassessment of catastrophe risk, but regulators approved only a 7.3 percent increase. In 1996, ISO filed for a 4.4 percent decrease and regulators

[19] See Conning & Company (1998) for a comparison of state regulatory environments for insurance.

imposed a 4.9 percent decrease. Hence, while we see some evidence of rate suppression in New York, it appears to be much less restrictive than that in Florida. This is not surprising given that catastrophe risk and cost pressures are less severe in New York than in Florida.

Rate compression in New York also differs from that in Florida, as revealed in Figures 3.3(a)–3.3(c). In 1992, for all but a handful of territories in New York there is little discernable difference between indicated and approved loss costs. These disparities increased in 1994, particularly for the highest cost territories. By 1996, the disparities more or less shrank to their 1992 levels. This is consistent with a pattern of limited rate compression found in many states, but not the kind of severe rate compression that we see in Florida. We should note that the range of indicated loss costs between high and low-cost territories is much smaller in New York than in Florida. The relatively small differences between indicated loss costs for high-cost territories and indicated loss costs for low-cost territories in New York suggests that regulators in the state were not subject to the same political pressure to compress rates as regulators in Florida.

Further, unlike Florida, New York did not impose a moratorium on policy cancellations and non-renewals. However, regulators did slow policy terminations in high-risk areas and established a Market Assistance Plan (MAP) to help homeowners find coverage with another insurer.[20] New York also has a general restriction on policy terminations to two percent of an insurer's exposures in a given year. This allows insurers to gradually adjust their portfolios of exposures, recognizing that there was probably less of a need to do so in New York than in Florida.

New York has a FAIR Plan that serves a residual market of last resort for homeowners unable to obtain insurance in the voluntary market. The New York FAIR Plan grew after 1992, but at a much slower pace than residual market mechanisms in Florida (see Figure 3.4(b)). The New York Plan appeared to have reached a plateau at around 87,900 policies and $10 billion in exposures in 1998. By year-end 2000, these figures dropped to 69,900 and $8.5 billion, respectively. New York does not have a wind pool akin to Florida's, nor has it instituted a catastrophe insurance or reinsurance facility, although the concept has received some discussion. It is likely that other factors, such as underwriting risks in urban areas, play a more important role in the New York FAIR Plan than in the Florida JUA.

New York is the only state with a pre-funded guaranty association for property-liability insurance. The association is authorized to assess member insurers' premiums up to two percent annually to maintain a certain fund balance. In the event of insolvencies and the resulting costs, this fund would

[20] Florida also has a MAP for homeowners insurance but the success of a MAP will be affected by regulatory rate suppression and compression.

be tapped and, if necessary, replenished through further assessments on insurers. Consequently, with the exception of its pre-funding requirement, New York's guaranty association would operate much like guaranty associations in other states in the event of a mega-catastrophe.[21] As in Florida, insurers surviving the initial flood of claims from a New York catastrophe would still be subject to the residual risk of catastrophe-related guaranty fund assessments. This would increase financial demands on surviving insurers.

---

[21] It could be argued that the pre-funding aspect of New York's guaranty association would have a temporal smoothing effect on catastrophe-related assessments. However, any such effect would likely be dwarfed in the event of a mega-catastrophe.

Chapter 4

SUPPLY, DEMAND AND REGULATION OF CATASTROPHE INSURANCE

This chapter provides a theoretical foundation for the empirical work to follow in the next chapter. We begin with a model of insurer decisions for a privately owned, profit-maximizing insurer. The model emphasizes the determination of an appropriate capital structure for the insurance firm to cover a specific set of geographically diversified exposures. To guard against the entry of poorly capitalized insurers, and for other demand-side reasons, insurance regulators oversee the entry, price structure and solvency of insurers. To motivate our empirical analysis in Chapter 5, we analyze the effects of such regulation on a typical insurer.

We then consider the structure of demand for catastrophe insurance. We begin with a brief examination of the problems confronting consumers of catastrophe insurance, highlighting some recognized behavioral anomalies in consumer purchase decisions for both insurance protection and the substitute good of other ex ante protective activities such as structural mitigation measures. This leads us to a discussion of the underlying theory of insurance pricing and the structure of the demand equations for bundled homeowners policies that will serve as the foundation for our empirical analysis in Chapter 5.

1. THE SUPPLY OF CATASTROPHE INSURANCE

This section illustrates the tradeoffs for insurers in catastrophe insurance markets where there may be significant regulatory constraints preventing optimal adjustment of the insurers' portfolios. We frame the analysis in terms of a solvency-constrained, expected profit maximizing insurer model for a specific insurer (the model dates from Stone, 1973). The model captures several tradeoffs. The level of the solvency constraint itself reflects the insurer's appetite for risk and, in particular, the tradeoff between the costs of increased surplus and the franchise value of the firm going forward, which is put at risk under insolvency. For any specific target level of insolvency probability, maximizing expected returns from a given equity base implies that the insurer will attempt to market its risk coverage to a geographically diversified portfolio of risks. On the other hand, scale economies in marketing, distribution and claims processing may drive the company to market more intensively in some areas than in others, leading to increased (positive) correlation among the risks in the insurer's portfolio. The model thus is intended to embody the interaction of demand and marketing payoffs relative to the costs of the capital required to support the book of business chosen by the insurer. These tradeoffs will be further complicated if regulators contravene adequate rates or cause cross-subsidies through rate compression.[1]

1.1 The Solvency-Constrained Insurer's Problem

Fix attention on a particular insurer in a specified region, e.g., the State of Florida. Denote by $x = (x_1, x_2, ..., x_n)$ the vector of exposures for the insurer, where x_i is the insurer's exposure in insurance zone i in the region. In keeping with the notion that the insurance market is workably competitive, we assume that the firm is a price-taker in the market, with price in zone i per unit of exposure given by p_i. Let $L_i(x_i)$ be the random variable representing losses in zone i and let $L(x) = L_1(x_1) + L_2(x_2) + ... + L_n(x_n)$ denote total losses. Losses in different zones may be correlated since the same event could create losses in more than one zone. Losses to different properties within a zone are correlated for the same reason. These losses may arise from catastrophe-affected lines of business or from other lines. We return below to the interaction effects of multi-peril coverages.

Denote by $\Pi(x, A, K)$ the expected profits for the insurer for a typical year, where A are the assets of the insurer supporting the business x and K is additional risk-bearing capital described in more detail below. We write expected profits as:

$$\begin{aligned}\Pi(x,A,K) &= R(x) - M(x) - \overline{L}^*(x,A,K) - rK = \\ &\sum_{i=1}^{n}\left[R_i(x_i) - M_i(x_i)\right] - \overline{L}^*(x,A,K) - rK\end{aligned} \tag{1}$$

[1] "Rate compression" is the term we use to label regulatory restrictions on the rate differential between low and high-risk insureds, which is typically imposed by capping the rates of high-risk insureds below their cost of risk.

where

$R_i(x_i)$ = Annual revenue from zone $_i$ = $p_i x_i$

$M_i(x_i)$ = Marketing, Sales and Distribution (annual) Expenses for zone i

$L^*(x, A, K) = E\{Min [L(x), (R(x) - M(x) + (1-r)K + A)]\}$ = Expected annual losses from all zones, truncated at the insolvency point L*, given by:

$$L^* = R(x) - M(x) + (1-r)K + A.$$

rK = Payments to capital providers for K

Marketing expenses M_i will depend on company organizational variables such as its distribution system. We will think of K as reinsurance, but K could also be in the form of zero-coupon bonds. The important assumption we make about K is that the premium (or interest in the case of bonds) is prepaid, before losses are known, so that (1-r)K is actually available to pay losses if K units of reinsurance are purchased. The shareholder equity A that the insurer puts at risk may influence the rate r or the amount of reinsurance K obtainable. We take A and r as fixed here and assume that K is set to just satisfy a solvency constraint, specified below. Once A and K are exhausted, i.e., insolvency occurs, the insurer bears no further responsibilities for losses; losses are therefore accounted for in the expected profit function only up to the point of insolvency.[2]

Thus, in the spirit of Herring and Vankudre (1987) and Greenwald and Stiglitz (1990), based on the transactions costs of insolvency and the franchise value of the firm going forward, solvency constraints may be viewed as an endogenous outcome of the options value of continued operations. The price of the option in this case is the differential returns to capital devoted to the insurance business at the margin rather than to other market opportunities. An alternative and equivalent approach to making insolvency probabilities endogenous, driven by an exogenously specified franchise value of the firm going forward, is to take the level of insolvency probability as exogenous. This is the approach we take here. In the language of Herring and Vankudre (1987), go-for-broke or gambling behavior corresponds to relatively high values of insolvency probability (reflecting for such firms low values of anticipated growth opportunities which cannot be converted to cash if insolvency occurs). Such behavior is to

---

2 In the corporate form of organization employed by all U.S. insurance companies, only owners' equity stake (including the franchise value of the firm) in the corporation is at risk – owners' other assets cannot be reached to satisfy unfunded liabilities of the corporation.

be contrasted with that of insurers with long-run profit prospects who would choose lower values of target insolvency probabilities reflecting the higher franchise of the firm going forward.[3]

These considerations lead to a model in which the insurer chooses its book of business x to maximize Π(x, A, K) subject to a solvency constraint based on a probable maximum loss (PML). This requires that underlying reserves and reinsurance A + (1-r)K be set large enough to avoid financial distress with a probability exceeding 1 - ρ, where ρ represents the worst case or PML probability. Formally, we have the following requirement:

$$\begin{aligned}&\Pr\{L(x) > R(x) - M(x) + (1-r)K + A\} = \\ &\qquad 1 - F[R(x) - M(x) + (1-r)K + A; x] \le \rho\end{aligned} \tag{2}$$

where F(L; x) = Pr{L(x) ≤ L} is the cumulative distribution function (cdf) of the total loss distribution. The import of (2) is the following. The probability that the insurer will be unable to cover losses (from revenues R(x),surplus (A), and reinsurance (1-r)K) of its policyholders after paying marketing expenses M(x) is no greater than the prespecified insolvency probability ρ. The insurer's problem of interest is to choose x to maximize (1) subject to (2). It will be convenient to reformulate this problem by defining the "net surplus function" S(x, ρ) as the unique solution to

$$F(S(x,\rho);x) = 1 - \rho \tag{3}$$

Using (3), we can state the problem of maximizing expected profits (1) subject to the solvency constraint (2) succinctly as:

$$Maximize\left[R(x) - M(x) - \overline{L}^{*} - rK \;\middle|\; R(x) - M(x) + (1-r)K + A \ge S(x,\rho)\right] \tag{4}$$

Intuitively, S(x, ρ) is the amount of capital from all sources required to assure that the probability the insurer's losses in a given period exceed S will be no greater than ρ. Alternatively, S(x, ρ) specifies the amount of surplus required to avoid financial distress with probability 1-ρ. The net surplus S(x, ρ) is increasing in both expected losses and the variance of total losses. To the extent that losses across zones are positively correlated, as might be

[3] Under "normal" circumstances, several stakeholder groups have reasons to limit the insolvency probability of an insurance firm. These stakeholders include owners, policyholders, other insurer creditors, and regulators. However, sometimes insurance companies encounter substantial financial difficulty and employ a "go-for-broke" strategy before regulators and the market become aware of the hazardous condition of the firm.

expected for neighboring zones, the variance in total losses will increase further. Meeting the solvency constraint (2) means putting enough premium revenue and capital behind the portfolio to assure assets of S(x, ρ) to meet losses. The characteristics of the portfolio are clearly important in determining S(x, ρ) -- the more highly correlated they are, the larger the required surplus.

Associating the shadow price $\lambda \geq 0$ with the constraint in (4), we obtain the following first-order conditions (FOCs) for optimal exposures x for the insurer's problem[4]:

$$\frac{\partial \Pi(x, A, K)}{\partial x_i} = \frac{\lambda}{1+\lambda}\left[\frac{\partial S(x,\rho)}{\partial x_i}\right] \tag{5}$$

By the definition of $\bar{L}^*(x, A, K)$, one readily verifies that $\partial \bar{L}^*(x, A, K)/\partial K = (1-r)\rho$. Thus, the FOC for optimal capital K* in (4) yields $\lambda = \rho + r/(1-r)$, so that defining $\beta(r, \rho) = [\rho(1-r) + r]/[\rho(1-r) + 1]$, we have $\beta(r, \rho) = \lambda/(1+\lambda)$. Note that $\beta(r, \rho) \rightarrow r$ as $\rho \rightarrow 0$. Then, given our assumption that A is fixed, the optimal K* will be set to just achieve equality in (2) at the x* determined by (5).

Under regularity assumptions on the concavity and smoothness of the profit function, decreasing the required level of insolvency probability ρ will, as expected, reduce the optimal book of business everywhere. To see this, assume that the expected profit function is concave for x > 0, although there may be discontinuities at $x_i = 0$, resulting for example from the fixed costs of setting up infrastructure to market in zone i. Assuming exposures give rise to losses that are positively interdependent, decreasing ρ will increase the magnitude of the quantity in brackets in (3).[5] Given this fact,

4 The Lagrangean for the optimization problem in (6) is just $\mathcal{L}(x, \lambda) = [R(x) - M(x) - \bar{L}^*(x,A,K) - rK] + \lambda[R(x) - M(x) + (1-r)K + A - S(x, \rho)]$. Taking derivatives and simplifying leads directly to (5).

5 By positive interdependence, we mean that if exposures y (additional insured properties) are added to a book of business x, then $\Pr\{L(x+y) = L(x) + L(y) \leq L \mid L(y) = L_0\}$ is non-decreasing in L_0. By definition of the net surplus function S, we have $\Pr\{L(x+y) \leq S(x+y, \rho)\} = \Pr\{L(x) \leq S(x, \rho)\} = 1-\rho$, so that S(x+y, ρ) and S(x, ρ) are the (1-ρ)th upper fractile of the cdf of L(x+y) and L(x) respectively. Given the positive interdependence between L(x) and L(y), the asserted monotonicity states that the difference between this fractile and the mean of the distribution is increasing as exposures increase. The most intuitive example of this is the normal distribution. In this case, $S(x+y, \rho) = E\{L(x+y)\} + k(\rho)\sigma(L(x+y))$, so that $S(x+y, \rho) - E\{L(x+y)\} = k(\rho)\sigma(L(x+y))$ which is clearly increasing in y for any given x; i.e., since L(x) and L(y) are not negatively correlated, as more exposures are added the variance of the loss distribution of the overall portfolio of business increases.

and noting that expected profits are separable across zones, (5) implies that the book of business x_i will be reduced in each zone for which $x_i > 0$ obtains in the unconstrained expected profit maximizing solution. In fact, the book of business will be scaled down in each zone to a level that depends on how sensitive increases in net surplus over expected losses are to changes in exposure in the zone. This, in turn, will depend on the degree of correlation of the losses within zone i to intrazonal and interzonal losses. Intuitively, the higher the correlation, the larger the impact on the right hand tail of the joint distribution of L(x) and the higher the marginal net surplus requirements $\partial S(x, \rho)/\partial x_i$ over $\partial \bar{L}^*(x, A, K)/\partial x_i$.

1.2 Price Regulation

Regulation interacts with the above analysis in several ways, including determination of required solvency levels (1-ρ), price and profit constraints, underwriting constraints, and entry and exit constraints (see Klein, 1998b).[6] All of these can be important in shaping the market outcome for catastrophe insurance. We discuss only the effects of price constraints here, leaving to a discussion below the effects of other regulatory constraints.

To model the effects of price constraints, assume the regulator imposes constraints of the form $p_i \le P_i$, i = 1, 2, ..., n. From (5), there will be a direct effect of these price ceilings on the optimal coverages x_i^* the insurer can offer in zone i. Indeed, rewriting (5) to separate the marginal effects of revenue and marketing costs, we obtain:

$$p_i = \frac{\partial M_i(x_i)}{\partial x_i} + \frac{\partial \bar{L}^*(x, A, K)}{\partial x_i} + \beta(r, \rho)\left[\frac{\partial S(x, \rho)}{\partial x_i}\right] \qquad (6)$$

Assuming that the right-hand side of (6) is increasing in x_i, it is clear that decreases in the allowed price p_i must result in decreases in coverage in zone i. The erosion in profits implied by pricing constraints will be both the direct effects through price ceilings and the indirect effects through decreased contributions from zone i to the company's overall net surplus requirements. A possible strategy for the insurer would be exit from the high risk, price-regulated zones, but this may be further constrained by the regulator.[7]

6 There is an obvious conflict between regulators' political and/or ideological motivation to maintain low rates, ensure availability of coverage, and limit insurers' insolvency risk (see Klein, 1998b).

7 Indeed, let us think of the x vector above as having two entries for each actual insurance zone, the first being for non-catastrophe exposures and the second for cat exposures in the

1.3 A Two-Zone Example

To make the above analysis more concrete, we briefly consider an example in which there are only two zones, i = 1,2.[8] We are interested in the interacting effects of correlated demand on the net surplus and on possible economies of scale in marketing on total expenses at the solvency constrained optimal solution. Let the functions R, M, L and S be specified as follows:

$$R_i(x_i) = p_i x_i$$

$$M_i(x_i) = m_i\ \delta(x_i) + b_i x_i^2, \text{ where } \delta(y) = 1 \text{ for } y > 0 \text{ and } 0 \text{ otherwise}$$

$$\bar{L}_i(x_i) = E\{L_i(x_i)\} = c_i x_i$$

$$S(x, \rho) = \bar{L}(x) + k(\rho)(h_1 x_{12} + h_2 x_{22})^{.5}$$

where m_i, b_i, c_i, $h_i > 0$ are constants and $k(\rho)$ is decreasing in ρ. The function $S(x, \rho)$ is motivated by the fractiles of the normal distribution together with an assumption that the coefficient of variation of total losses $L_i(x_i)$ in each zone is a constant. To simplify, assume that ρ is sufficiently small that $\bar{L}^*(x) \cong \bar{L}(x)$ and $\beta(r, \rho) \cong r$. Then, defining $a_i = p_i - c_i$, and assuming $a_i > 0$, expected profits can be expressed as:

$$\Pi(x, A, K) = \sum_{i=1}^{2}\left(a_i x_i - m_i \delta(x_i) - b_i x_i^2\right) - rK \qquad (7)$$

---

same zone, and let us imagine a scenario in which there are demand synergies from offering multi-peril (bundled) coverages. In the case of bundled products (where marketing of cat and non-cat perils occurs jointly, e.g., though a multi-peril homeowners policy), increases in exposure would be pursued until net revenues from the bundled coverage were equilibrated at the margin against additional marketing and surplus costs, as required by (6). That is to say, one would simply reinterpret (6) as the price for the bundled coverage (with x being the sum of both components of exposure). If regulatory policy contravenes adequate rates for the cat coverage, insurers might still issue bundled policies that satisfy the above constraint on exposures, but in this case the non-cat revenues would be cross-subsidizing the cat risks. Clearly, absent regulatory restrictions or demand synergies, competition would assure the collapse of the market for catastrophe coverage when rates are inadequate. Absent the assured hostage of earnings from the non-cat coverage, insurers would be forced to exit the cat market in these inadequate rate zones. This would be further exacerbated if cat and non-cat coverage could not unbundled because either of regulatory prohibitions or consumer demands for bundled coverage.

8 Given our interest in the tail events driving insolvency, we refer to this example as "The Tail of Two Cities".

If $x_i > 0$, then substituting the above expressions in the first-order condition (5) implies that

$$a_i - 2b_i x_i = \frac{rk(\rho)h_i x_i}{\left(h_1 x_1^2 + h_2 x_2^2\right)^{1/2}} \; ; i = 1,2 \tag{8}$$

with the optimal capital K* set to just achieve equality in (2) at the x* determined by (8). Serving zone i at exposure levels x_i* would be optimal if sufficient expected profits are generated in zone i at this solution to balance the fixed cost m_i of establishing marketing infrastructure in zone i. Otherwise, the insurer will pull out of zone i (i.e., set $x_i = 0$).

Consider the effect of insolvency constraints for this case. From (8) and $a_i = p_i - c_i$, if $x_i > 0$ at optimum then reducing p_i will reduce the righthand side of (8). But the right-hand side of (8) is easily shown to be increasing in x_i. Thus, the optimal solution to (8) decreases if the regulated rate ceiling P_i is decreased. If the rate ceiling P_i for is set low enough, and absent exit restrictions, the fixed cost m_i of infrastructure for zone i would not be recovered and the insurer would exit zone i altogether. For the above model, exit restrictions in the form of constraints $x_i \geq \underline{x}_i$ (i.e., floors, perhaps based on historical exposure levels) would have the direct effect of suppressing profits from operations in zone i and the indirect effect of suppressing coverage in other zones since the profits from zone i are used in part to provide the net surplus required for overall operations. Thus, coupling exit restrictions with price ceilings would have the anticipated double impact on the zones in which they applied and, through net surplus erosion, on overall coverage.

Summarizing the insights from this analysis, we see the following. As the solvency constraint becomes more stringent (i.e., as ρ decreases in (2)), insurers facing no price or exit restrictions will decrease their exposures. How fast exposures x_i will be reduced in each zone depends on marginal marketing and distribution costs and the magnitude of net surplus required over expected losses. If x_i falls far enough, a particular zone may fail to meet the *ex ante* profit threshold for establishing marketing and distribution infrastructure, thus leading companies to be represented in some zones and not others. Profits and presence thus depend in essential ways on the structure of spatially determined costs. For example, it is well known (see Berger, Cummins and Weiss, 1997) that direct writers face cost structures with larger fixed costs m_i and lower variable costs bi than agency writers.[9]

---

9 "Direct writers" must establish their own distribution system, whereas "agency" insurers utilize an existing system of independent agents. Note that independent agents are

One consequence of this is that, for companies of equal size, we would expect direct writers to exhibit higher variance in both their presence and their exposures across zones than agency writers.

The key elements driving the structure of optimal insurance portfolios for private insurers involve complex tradeoffs between the drivers of net surplus required to assure solvency criteria are met, and the structure of regulated prices across zones and marketing cost functions. It is therefore not surprising, in light of this complexity, that risk modeling companies have assumed such an important role in assisting insurers in the evaluation of the pricing, profit and solvency impacts of their exposures.[10] It is perhaps more surprising that regulators in some jurisdictions have attempted micro-management of prices and exit restrictions, notwithstanding the complexity of these matters for individual insurers.[11] For example, as we explored in Chapters 2 and 3, and as we will further explore in Chapter 5, the combination of price and entry restrictions in Florida have led to underpricing of the risks, distorted entry decisions, and dissatisfaction by insurers in that state. Underpricing of risks undoubtedly also promoted inefficient mitigation choices as noted above. While some of these problems have been slowly ameliorated over time, the Florida example underlines the key insight that over regulation of catastrophe insurance markets can have multiple negative consequences.[12]

2. THE STRUCTURE OF DEMAND FOR HOMEOWNERS INSURANCE

2.1 The Basic Economic Model

The demand for insurance enjoys a long literature in general (e.g., Arrow, 1971; Dionne and Harrington, 1992) and for catastrophe loss in particular (e.g., Kunreuther, 1998b; Palm, 1998). In the simplest case, a potential

---

typically able to demand higher commissions than exclusive agents employed by direct writers. This leads to the differences in the fixed and variable costs involved with the two different approaches.

10 For an introduction to risk modeling techniques, the reader is referred to the earlier discussion in Chapter 2 and the Appendix.

11 Insurance regulators can impede an insurer's exit from a market through a number of devices. This is done to strengthen regulators' ability to enforce binding price constraints.

12 As our empirical analysis indicates, regulators allowed insurers to gradually raise their rates in Florida to reflect revised, higher expected losses. However, rates in the most catastrophe-vulnerable areas were not allowed to rise to adequate levels and recent media accounts indicate that regulators are opposing further rate increases.

insurance buyer can undertake ex ante protective care (think of this as structural mitigation measures to reinforce the soundness of the buyer's building so as to reduce the losses from natural hazards). The cost of such mitigation measures is denoted by z. The buyer can also purchase insurance coverage. Thereafter, the buyer faces a loss L(z) that can occur in a particular period (say a year) with a probability $r(z) \in (0, 1)$, and a loss of 0 with probability 1 – r(z). We assume that insurance is offered at a cost of "c" per unit (e.g., per $) of coverage M purchased (where we assume losses are only covered up to the level of the loss). Assuming the buyer has preferences that can be represented by expected utility, the buyer will undertake protective activity $z \geq 0$ and purchase coverage $M \geq 0$ so as to maximize:

$$V(x, M) = r(z)U(W - cM - z + Min(M, L(z)) - L(z))$$

$$+ \ (1-r(z))U(W - cM - z) \qquad (9)$$

where W is the buyer's initial wealth. Since our focus here is on natural hazards, we assume r(z) = r, independent of z. Then, assuming that L(z) is monotonic decreasing and convex in protective activity x and that U(W) is concave and increasing in wealth W, maximization of (9) is easily seen to imply that no more than full coverage will be purchased, $M \leq L(z)$.

Now assume that insurance premiums satisfy the viability condition $c \geq r$ for non-negative profits for the insurer. From this, it follows that if full coverage is taken $(M = L(z))$, then $L'(z) = dL/dz = -1/c \geq -1/r$ at optimum. In the absence of insurance (M = 0), the buyer with preferences as given in (9) would set z such that

$$-L'(z) = \frac{rU'(W - z - L(z)) + (1 - r)U'(W - z)}{rU'(W - z - L(z))} < \frac{1}{r} \qquad (10)$$

where the inequality follows from the assumed concavity of U. The availability of insurance decreases the incentives for mitigation/ex ante protective activity (i.e., moral hazard exists here). More generally, comparative statics for the solution to (9) show that the optimal x satisfies $z'(c) > 0$ (so that the higher the price of insurance, the stronger the incentives for mitigation). Note, however, that the socially optimal level of protective care minimizes $z + rL(z)$ (i.e., $L'(z) = -1/r$), so that when insurance is too expensive to purchase any coverage, (10) implies that the risk-averse expected utility maximizer will actually mitigate more than what would be socially efficient. A number of wrinkles can be added to (9)-(10), such as deductibles, non-linear contracts, misperceptions by the buyer of probabilities or losses, etc. See Kunreuther (1996, 1998b) for some of these.

While the above theory has served economics well in motivating research on insurance markets, it has become clear through empirical research that the model embodied in (9)-(10) is not satisfactory as a model of the actual behavior of insurance buyers, especially for catastrophe insurance. As Kunreuther (1996, 1998b) notes, potential insurance buyers tend to be myopic and uninformed (about probabilities, losses and types of coverage available) in their purchase of both insurance coverage and mitigation measures. The consequence of these interacting effects is typically that these consumers do nothing before the event and plead for government assistance after the event. This has given rise in many countries to compulsory insurance and building codes in hazard-prone areas in order to encourage some minimal level of insurance coverage and the adoption of reasonable structural standards when they would prefer not to do so in the absence of such regulations.[13] If coverage regulations are to make sense economically, they cannot be arbitrary, of course. In particular, pricing for mandated coverages must reflect economically sensible, i.e., risk-based prices, and building codes must reflect cost-effective mitigation measures, requirements whose expected reductions in losses over time can cover the upfront costs of such measures. In addition to these issues on the demand side, the design of such regulations has to confront significant complexities on the supply side.

2.2 Demand Modeling for Homeowners When Insurance is Mandatory

The focus of our empirical work in the next chapter is on multi-peril homeowners policies, so we devote the remainder of this chapter to a discussion of this specific topic. There are several features of the market for homeowners insurance that constrain and structure the analysis of demand. First, we assume that homeowners insurance, including coverage against windstorm damage, is essentially mandatory for most homeowners, although some homeowners may elect a "no coverage" policy, i.e., they have no property insurance.[14] Consider this "no coverage" option as purchasing an

---

[13] See, e.g., Kleindorfer and Kunreuther (1999) and Grace, Klein and Kleindorfer (1999, 2000) for details on regulatory initiatives adopted in the U.S. for insurance and mitigation. See also Kleindorfer and Sertel (2001) for a discussion of similar themes in Turkey and elsewhere internationally.

[14] Lenders typically require hazard insurance for homes with mortgages. It is possible that some homeowners without a mortgage have opted not to purchase insurance. We control

insurance product with "infinite deductibles" at a price of zero. Also, coverage for wind may be excluded from a policy. Second, as assumed in our supply side analysis in 4 (§1) and as a number of previous analyses have shown (e.g., Joskow, 1973; and Grace, Klein and Kleindorfer, 1998; Cummins, Weiss and Zi, 1999), the market for homeowners insurance products is workably competitive.[15]

The consumer choice problem facing the homeowner is to select a single optimal policy from among the menu of policies offered in the market. This involves a complex tradeoff among the various attributes of the coverages purchased, the characteristics and needs of the homeowner, and the perceived quality of the companies from which coverage can be purchased. Demand in this market arises from the optimal consumer choice of a bundle of product and company attributes, given the personal characteristics of each homeowner and the economic and demographic characteristics of the neighborhood (i.e., represented here by the homeowner's Zip code) where he resides. The feasible set of such "bundled products" is the set of insurance policies, coverage options, and company attributes that can be sustained in a competitive equilibrium under regulatory constraints such as those discussed in Chapters 2 and 3.

The theoretical foundation for this demand analysis, and the interacting market equilibrium, are based on a model of price-quality competition (e.g., Gal-or, 1983). In a competitive market, the differences in what homeowners are willing to pay for various insurance policy features will be reflected in the prices at which various bundled products with these features sell. Thus, what we will model in the next chapter is essentially a regression of observed prices in the market against various features of the products sold and the companies that sell them. We are interested in the factors that appear to influence demand and whether these factors appear reasonable on the basis of theory. Since there is considerable evidence that many homeowners do not search thoroughly for "best offers", we are also interested in market phenomena that appear to arise from behavioral considerations, including the

---

for this in the models below using Census data (as of 1990) on the percent of homeowners having mortgages in each ZIP code represented in our sample. Insurers typically require homeowner to insure 80 percent (or more) of the value of real estate (as the land is not insurable). It is quite possible that people might still have mortgage payments to make, but opt out of insurance because the mortgage is less than 20 percent of the property's value.

[15] The standard structural and performance benchmarks discussed in Chapter 2, such as concentration measures and various financial indicators of profitability, also support this statement.

price dispersion of similar policies offered in the same geographic area (e.g., Kunreuther, 1998b).[16]

We assume that the set of policies offered by companies, together with their underwriting and marketing strategies, are expected profit maximizing, subject to imposed regulatory constraints. This suggests that companies find the regulatory policies imposed not so onerous as to cause them to leave the market. Nonetheless, as discussed in Chapter 4 (§1) and in Chapter 3 (§2), because of regulatory constraints, catastrophe coverages in some areas might require "underbracing" or cross subsidies from other lines of business, non-catastrophe coverages or catastrophe coverages in other areas.[17] These cross subsidies may be sustainable in equilibrium if they allow insurance companies to earn a reasonable rate of return on all lines of business and if they are supported by consumer preferences for certain feature bundles and companies because of their reputation.[18] The continuation of these cross subsidies over time implies some further inertia that may, at least in part, be due to regulatory restrictions on terminating policies and other insurer and consumer considerations, such as cross marketing of insurance products within the same company.[19]

2.3 Defining Price and Modeling Demand for Homeowner Policies

Assume that a particular homeowner, with characteristics Z (income, family status, type of structure, etc.), faces a choice among different policy options for insuring his home, where the set H gives the available policy options in the homeowners market. A typical such option "h" in the set H would be one offered by firm i (with characteristics X_i) with certain policy

[16] We should note that one source of price dispersion is the fact that insurance companies differentiate themselves in term of underwriting stringency. Insurers with more stringent underwriting standards, labeled "preferred insurers," tend to have the lowest prices. "Standard" and "non-standard" companies tend to have less stringent underwriting standards and higher prices. Some insureds may pay higher than necessary prices if they would qualify for coverage from a preferred insurer, but intentionally or inadvertently purchase coverage from a standard or non-standard insurer.

[17] To the extent that catastrophe insurance is cross subsidized, the incentives to mitigate catastrophe losses are undermined. Other social costs include sub-optimal purchases of insurance for the lines or areas providing the subsidies.

[18] For example, insurers may also offer auto insurance and even life insurance policies to their homeowners insureds. This will affect their incentives to terminate homeowners insureds due to regulatory pricing constraints.

[19] See Bartlett, Klein and Russell (1999) for a discussion of how regulation-imposed insurance price subsidies may be sustained for a period of time.

features such as deductible levels, loss settlement provisions (i.e., actual cash value or replacement cost on contents), and the premium *P(h)*. The homeowner must choose one of the options in *H* and does so by maximizing his expected utility over the risks or "gambles" implied by each choice *h*. We represent this expected utility *U(h, P(h))* in quasi-linear form as:[20]

$$U(h, P(h), Z) = V(F(h), Z) - P(F(h), Z) \quad (11)$$

where *V* represents, for a consumer of type *Z*, the consumer's willingness to pay for various coverages or "features" of an insurance policy and *F(h)* represents the vector of such features, including the characteristics of the company offering the policy that may make a difference to consumers. Note that both *V* and *P* are shown to depend only on the vector of features *F* and the characteristics of the homeowner (where homeowner characteristics could include the type of structure, as well as the homeowner's locational characteristics such as the "protection classification" assigned to fire and police services in the area). The homeowner then maximizes the function *U(h, P(h), Z)* over the set *H*. Assuming that the policy features can be more or less continuously varied (that is, there is a rich menu of policies available in the market), we can represent the choice problem as choosing an insurance policy by choosing optimal features of the policy. This leads to a solution to the homeowner's maximization problem characterized by $\partial V/\partial F_i = \partial P/\partial F_i$, which varies with consumer characteristics *Z*. From this logic, one can understand the structure of demand in this market by examining how premiums vary with policy features.[21] This leads to estimation problems of the following general type, neglecting for the moment the details of functional form:

$$P(F, X, Z) = aF + bX + cZ + \varepsilon \quad (12)$$

In this model, *P(F, X, Z)* could be either the total premium for a given policy or more preferably, normalizing by units of coverage (e.g., the expected or indicated loss costs), the price per unit of coverage.

---

[20] As Willig (1976) has shown, this form, with constant marginal utility of income, is appropriate for demand modeling when the good in question does not constitute a significant portion of the homeowner's budget, a reasonable assumption in the case of insurance (the typical homeowners insurance premium is around \$400-\$600 and somewhat higher in catastrophe-prone areas). This is not to say, of course, that there are no income effects across consumers, only that the marginal utility of income for each consumer is assumed constant over the range of policy options offered.

[21] Indeed, if V and P are estimated using bilinear or translog families of functions, then knowledge of one will lead (up to a constant of integration) to knowledge of the other.

The "price" for insurance products, as for other products and services, is defined on the basis of value-added per unit (in this case, per dollar) of output. At the policy level, this value-added measure of price can be captured by subtracting the discounted value of expected losses covered by the policy from the policy's premium.[22] Denoting by *L(F, Z)* the expected losses for a policy *h* with features *F* in neighborhood z, and by *P(F, X, Z)* its premium, we obtain the following definition of price *p(F, X, Z)* for a homeowners policy *h = (F, X, Z)* characterized by the parameters *(F, X)* and indexed by consumer and loss characteristics *Z*:

$$p(F,X,Z) = \frac{P(F,X,Z) - PV((L(F,Z))}{PV(L(F,Z))} = \frac{(1+r)P(F,X,Z) - L(F,Z)}{L(F,Z)} \qquad (13)$$

where *PV(L(F, Z)) = L(F, Z)/(1+r)* is the present value of expected losses on the policy for the policy period and "*r*" is the insurer's return on investments for the period. *L(F,Z)* is the expected loss cost per unit of coverage for the policy features (*F*) and insured structure (*Z*). We will, in fact, directly estimate (13) using a functional form similar to (12). For the ISO database underlying this study, we have information on the premium charged for each policy (or group of identical policies), "*r*" is the average ratio of investment income to earned premiums for insurers, and *L(F, Z)* represents the advisory *Indicated Loss Costs* (ILCs), as computed using ISO filed loss cost manuals and rules, for the policy characteristics *(F, Z)*.[23]

We further analyze the indicated loss costs (ILCs). We employ the indicated loss costs for an insured property as a measure of real insurance services output. Using ISO loss cost filing information, we calculated an

---

22 Note that we do not consider the effects of taxes in this model. See Myers and Cohn (1987) and Cummins (1990) for a more detailed discussion of "price" in the insurance context. See also Cummins, Weiss and Zi (1999) for a related empirical study of price and profitability using frontier efficiency methods. As noted in the latter paper, the definition of price in equation (13) below properly accounts for the insurer's expenses and the opportunity costs of the owner's capital invested in the insurance business.

23 We discuss the ISO procedures in more detail in Chapter 5. For the moment, the reader should take these advisory Indicated Loss Costs as our best estimates of the expected annual costs resulting from policy features, structural characteristics and location of a property. The non-catastrophe portion of Indicated Loss Costs is based on actuarial experience and the catastrophe portion is based on catastrophe modeling results. As discussed below, the expected loss costs implied in individual insurers' prices could vary from the ISO Indicated Loss Costs, which represent overall industry projected costs. Also, it should be clear from the discussion of regulation in Chapter 3 that Indicated Loss Costs are not necessarily the same as the advisory loss costs approved by regulators.

expected indicated loss cost for each contract.[24] That is, ISO loss cost information can be used to determine the expected loss cost for a given homeowners policy form that covers a brick house in Zip code 30029 with certain specified coverage provisions and endorsements/exclusions, such as ordinance/law coverage. ISO also has provided information on indicated catastrophe loss costs and non-catastrophe loss costs that we have applied to each possible combination of location, policy form, and other contract terms. The catastrophe loss costs were estimated using a catastrophe model that provides location and structure-specific estimates of the expected losses to an insured property from the natural hazard in question (see Appendix B for details). Indicated loss costs, for both catastrophe coverage and non-catastrophe perils such as fire and theft, for a particular policy are an estimate of the expected claims costs (including loss adjustment expenses) of insurance coverage under the terms of that policy for a particular house. Thus, indicated loss costs are a proxy for the amount of insurance embodied in a specific policy. One might also employ the Coverage A limit as a proxy for the amount of insurance. However, while the Coverage A limit reflects the homeowners perceived value of the home, it does not necessarily reflect the risk of loss to the home.[25] It is essentially the maximum possible loss rather than the expected loss.[26] We therefore focus on indicated loss costs.

Three loss cost equations will be estimated. The first is for the catastrophe coverage and the second is for non-catastrophe coverage. The third combines both coverages. The equations are of the following general form:

$$L(F,Z)_{i=C,NC,TOT} = \beta_1 F + \beta_2 Z + \beta_3 X + \beta_4 P + e \qquad (14)$$

where $L(F, Z)_i$ reflects the quantity of real insurance services demanded, measured by the ILCs for catastrophe, non-catastrophe, or total coverage, F represents a vector of policy form/coverage terms, Z represents a vector of

[24] ISO advisory loss costs filings and associated information present indicated, filed and implemented (i.e., approved) loss costs for a "base" policy and a number of rating factors and rules that effectively enable one to calculate a loss cost for a particular policy, reflecting a set of standard coverage and risk characteristics.

[25] Insurers typically require homeowners to insure at least 70-80 percent of the insured value of their home (e.g., its market value or replacement cost) and are reluctant to sell coverage significantly exceeding market value or replacement cost. Most insurers use a model or formula to estimate the market value or replacement cost of a home.

[26] Actually, the maximum possible loss encompasses the limits of all non-liability coverages minus deductibles, but other coverage limits are typically stated as percentages of the Coverage A limit. The standard HO3 policy contains standard percentage limits for these other coverage, but insureds may select alternative limits.

insured/structure/neighborhood characteristics, X represents a vector of company characteristics, and P represents price.

These general forms of the Premium equation (12), the Price equation (13) and the Loss Cost equation (14) will serve as the basis for our estimation procedures. They incorporate both non-catastrophe perils and catastrophe perils or windstorms. The reader may think of these simply as separate features of a given policy. We are interested in identifying the effects of explanatory variables on the purchase of catastrophe and non-catastrophe coverages separately and combined.

3. SUMMARY

The received theory on factors influencing demand and supply of insurance products is rich and long, both in terms of the rational consumer and firm models reviewed earlier in this chapter as well as in behavioral and experimental studies of actual behavior. The basic theory recognizes that, through pooling, insurance provides a mechanism to reduce the volatility of losses at a price, the "risk premium" or loading, that risk averse consumers are prepared to pay. Competition then assures that the coverages that are provided in the market are produced efficiently, and at appropriate quality levels that trade off consumer willingness-to-pay to the marginal cost of quality increases. The result, in equilibrium is a set of products that minimize the total costs of providing desired coverages, including the cost of capital backing these policies.

Regulation can play a positive role in promoting this ideal state by discouraging gambling behavior by insurers who may otherwise offer policies that do not have requisite quality and capital backing. As we have seen in earlier chapters, however, the supply of and demand for catastrophe insurance is more complicated in reality than our stylized analytic models are likely to capture. This is especially true in areas like catastrophe insurance where understanding and evaluating the peril is difficult. Thus, we turn to the highlight of this monograph, the empirical assessment of the determinants of demand and the structure of pricing in two key states facing mixed catastrophe perils, Florida and New York.

Chapter 5

DEMAND ESTIMATION FOR HOMEOWNERS INSURANCE POLICIES

In this chapter we present estimates of the demand for homeowners insurance derived from two-stage least squares regressions for New York and Florida. We estimate the demand at the level of the Zip code. Because we have the Zip code location of the insured house and we have access to Zip code level information from the Census, we model the demand for coverage at the level of the Zip code.[1]

In Florida, we have approximately usable 663,500 house years for the four-year period 1995-1998 that are aggregated to approximately 40,000 unique observations by firm, policy type, and Zip Code. Some data were excluded due to incompatible records, the generation of new Zip codes over the reporting period (making their integration with collateral Census data difficult), and missing information on some records. For New York, there are 2,335,000 house years for the same four-year period. When these data are aggregated to the firm and Zip code level, it results in approximately 66,000 unique observations.

The dataset contains full homeowners' premium and exposure data for 60 companies, comprising some 20 groups, taken as a snapshot in the first quarter of each of the four years, 1995-1998. Each record contains "slightly aggregated" information on similar groups of policies in each Zip code in which reporting companies did business. The information contains data regarding the characteristics of the policies actually purchased by homeowners for each company, including premiums, structural information on the nature of the insured property, and coverages purchased. Additionally, we have compiled financial and organizational data on the insurers in our

---

[1] We recognize that some Zip codes are quite large geographically and many are diverse demographically, but this is the smallest level of aggregation that will permit analysis of our data.

sample (from the NAIC data tapes and A.M. Best.), as well as household economic and demographic data (from the 1990 Census) by Zip code.

Table 5.1

Comparison of Homeowners Contracts Basic Terms

Contract Terms ...	HO1 (sold in few states like NY)	HO2	HO3 Typical	HO5 Most Comprehensive	HO8
	Policy Form				
Insurance Covers ...	Named Perils Only	Named Perils Only	Everything Except Exclusions (all perils)	Everything Except Exclusions (all perils)	Named Perils Only
Home	X	X	X	X	X
Other Attached Property and Structures	X	X	X	X	X
Personal Property	X	X	X	X	X
Loss of Use	X	X	X	X	X
Personal Liability to Others	X	X	X	X	X
Medical Payments to Others	X	X	X	X	X
Replacement Cost Coverage or Repair (Dwelling)	Repair	Repair	Repair but Endorsement Available	Replace	Lesser of Repair, Replace, or Market Value
Replacement Cost Coverage or Repair (Contents)	Repair	Repair	Repair but Endorsement Available	Replace	Repair
Ordinance or Law Coverage	X*	X*	X*	X*	Not available
Off Premises Theft Coverage	X*	X*	X*	X*	Not available

*Additional coverage options available.

Source: Authors' analysis of Standard ISO Contracts for Florida and New York

Table 5.1 summarizes the contract policy features for various classes of policies sold in the market. It has coverages for the home and attached structures, detached structures, personal property, loss of use, personal liability, and medical payments to others. The HO5 policy offers broader coverage than an HO3 policy. The HO3 policy provides named-perils coverage for personal property; the HO5 policy provides open-perils coverage on personal property. It is possible to purchase an HO15 endorsement on an HO3 policy to replicate the coverage provided by an HO5 policy – we treat the HO3/HO15 combination as an HO5 policy. The third most relevant policy form HO8 covers a more limited set of named perils than HO3 policies. HO1 policies (sold in only a few states including New York) are similar to the HO8 policy, but do not cover personal property. The HO2 policy is more akin to the HO3 policy but does not cover personal property.

For certain contracts, consumers may choose to purchase actual cash value or replacement cost coverage on personal property. Ordinance or law coverage is typically chosen as an endorsement on HO3 policies while it is a standard coverage in HO5 policies.[2] Finally, there is a wind protection device credit that consumers in Florida can obtain if they install specified mitigation features, such as storm shutters or roof straps.

Table 5.2 shows descriptive statistics on the contracts in our data. We see that HO3 contracts make up the majority of contracts written in both states. Overall, HO3 contracts account for approximately 92 percent of all contracts written in Florida by our sample companies. The other policy forms account for the remainder of the transactions sampled. In New York, the same pattern is evident where HO3 is the most common contract. HO3 polices account for 71.9 percent followed by HO2 polices which account for 20.3 percent.

Table 5.2
Mean Prices and Premium Level for Various Policy Forms in New York and Florida

	Florida			
	HO2	HO3	HO5	HO8
No of Contracts	4,381	977,850	71,659	210
Percent of Contracts	0.42%	92.77%	6.80%	0.02%
Premium	$ 443.81	$ 704.17	$ 1,038.85	$ 490.53
Price	1.452	1.2682	1.0255	1.777

	New York			
	HO1*	HO2	HO3	HO5
No of Contracts	8,847	473,487	1,675,717	172,897
Percent of Contracts	0.38%	20.31%	71.89%	7.42%
Premium	.	$ 492.84	$ 639.59	$ 869.01
Price	.	2.047	1.634	1.308

*Premium and Price Data not reported in ISO Data.

[2] Ordinance or Law Coverage will upgrade a rebuilt house after a covered loss to the current building code. Without the coverage, the house will be "repaired" or rebuilt according to code only as long as doing so does not exceed the Coverage A limit on the policy.

Table 5.3a

Florida Descriptive Statistics

Variables	Mean	Std. Dev.	Min	Max
Insured Risk Characteristics				
% of Homes with Frame Construction	0.305	0.337	0.000	1.000
% of Homes with Brick Construction	0.690	0.338	0.000	1.000
Protection Code (1 Is Highest)	4.927	1.731	1.000	10.000
Contract Terms				
Total Indicated Loss Costs	$ 884.51	1102.030	$121.93	$26,567.09
Catastrophe Related Modeled Indicated Loss Costs	$509.73	859.337	$ 0	$21,962.30
Non-Catastrophe Indicated Loss Costs	$374.78	290.342	$87.63	$5,548.80
Log of (Price +1)	0.148	0.485	-3.515	1.591
Price + 1	1.292	0.575	0.030	4.911
% of HO3 Policies in Zip Code	88.90%	0.261	0.00%	100.00%
% of HO5 Polices in Zip Code	11.75%	0.266	0.00%	100.00%
% of Ho8 Policies in Zip Code	0.05%	0.016	0.00%	100.00%
% of Policies with Wind Exclusion (Fl Only)	1.58%	0.106	0.00%	100.00%
% of Policies with Replacement Cost Coverage	91.00%	0.199	0.00%	100.00%
% of Policies with Ord or Law Coverage	52.50%	0.463	0.00%	100.00%
Coverage A Limit	$140,527	91715.950	$12,000	$1,009,091
Wind Deductible	$741.54	1449.74	$100.00	$9,994.70
Fire Deductible	$379.80	158.976	$100.00	$1,200.00
% of Total Indicated Lost Costs That Are Due to Cat Costs	42.36%	0.228	0.00%	91.06%
% with Wind Protection Device Credit (Fl)	6.20%	0.206	0.00%	100.00%
Neighborhood Characteristics				
% of Implemented Loss Costs to Indicated Loss Costs	69.04%	0.065	47.80%	92.04%
Median Year of Construction in Zip	1974.320	8.008	1943.000	1988.000
% of Homes in Zip Code with a Mortgage	87.05%	0.0821	0.00%	100.00%
Leverage Ratio of Median Housing Costs to Median income	0.026	0.006	0.000	0.083
Leverage Ratio of Median Housing Costs to Median Home Value	0.009	0.001	0.000	0.024
Average Age of Pop in Zip Code	39.370	7.158	19.651	71.907
% of Households in Urban Areas	75.90%	0.3566	0.00%	100.00%
% of Persons in Zip Aged 65 Or Over	17.76%	0.112	0.00%	82.42%
Median Income	$29,629.40	9,650.77	$ 7,890.00	$78,668.00
Firm Characteristics				
Direct Writer	0.157	0.364	0.000	1.000
Stock Company	0.893	0.309	0.000	1.000
Auto Premiums Written by Company	$29,032,243	47,672,173	$0	$181,509,056
Life Premiums Written by Sister Company	$ 30,078,038	56,541,230	$0	$182,655,744
Total Assets of Company Selling Policy	$ 3,125,676,695	4,307,150,626	$34,816,452	$21,168,613,920
AM Best Rating of A+ or Higher	0.575	0.494	0.000	1.000
AM Best Rating of A	0.250	0.433	0.000	1.000
AM Best Rating of A-	0.156	0.363	0.000	1.000
AM Best Rating of B+	0.011	0.106	0.000	1.000
AM Best Rating of NR2	0.007	0.085	0.000	1.000
Time Indicators				
1995 Indicator				
1996 Indicator	0.251	0.434	0.000	1.000
1997 Indicator	0.257	0.437	0.000	1.000
1998 Indicator	0.266	0.442	0.000	1.000

N = 40,971

Table 5.3b

New York Descriptive Statistics

Variables	Mean	Std. Dev.	Min	Max
insured Risk Characteristics				
% of Homes With Frame Construction	88.69%	0.229	0.00%	100.00%
% of Homes With Brick Construction	11.18%	0.228	0.00%	100.00%
Protection Code (1 Is Highest)	643.65%	2.370	100.00%	10.000
Contract Terms				
Total indicated Loss Costs	$448.43	262.123	$102.82	$4,309.08
Catastrophe Related Modeled indicated Loss Costs	$41.33	102.178	$ 0.14	$1,909.33
Non-Catastrophe indicated Loss Costs	$407.10	227.753	$89.53	$4,242.24
"Price + 1"	1.725	0.549	0.137	4.974
% of HO1 Policies in Zip Code (Ny Only)	0.40%	0.032	0.00%	83.3%
% of HO2 Policies in Zip Code	17.75%	0.271	0.00%	100.0%
% of HO3 Policies in Zip Code	73.61%	0.316	0.00%	100.0%
% of HO5 Polices in Zip Code	8.24%	0.213	0.00%	100.0%
% of HO8 Policies in Zip Code	0.00%	0.004	0.00%	100.0%
% of Policies With Replacement Cost Coverage	67.21%	0.335	0.00%	100.0%
% of Policies With Ord Or Law Coverage	35.24%	0.444	0.00%	100.0%
Coverage A Limit	183.562	104.966	5.000	1009.090
Wind Deductible	327.023	160.558	0.000	1200.000
Fire Deductible	342.208	162.506	50.000	1200.000
% of Total indicated Lost Costs That Are Due to Cat Costs	6.86%	12.36%	0.02%	63.28%
% with Off Premises Theft Coverage	2.82%	12.01%	0.00%	100.00%
Neighborhood Characteristics				
% of Implemented Loss Costs to Indicated Loss Costs	91.95%	0.109	0.00%	110.74%
Median Year of Construction in Zip	1955.720	10.615	1939.000	1988.000
% of Homes in Zip Code With A Mortgage	79.60%	0.114	0.00%	100.00%
Leverage Ratio of Median Housing Costs to Median income	0.025	0.008	0.000	0.140
Leverage Ratio of Median Housing Costs to Median Home Value	0.007	0.002	0.000	0.037
Average Age of Persons in Zip Code	36.650	3.600	20.759	61.767
% of Households in Urban Areas	55.16%	0.497	0.00%	100.00%
% of Persons in Zip Aged 65 Or Over	13.51%	0.050	0.00%	67.74%
Median income	$40,004.39	16663.760	$4,999.00	$150,001.00
Firm Characteristics				
Direct Writer	0.134	0.341	0.000	1.000
Stock Company	0.902	0.297	0.000	1.000
Auto Premiums Written by Company	$44,084,866	40809184	$526	$152,694,176
Life Premiums Written by Sister Company	$193,270,586	289152435	$3,436	$904,290,112
Total Assets of Company Selling Policy	$3,120,947,934	3750565022	$19,213,992	$20,535,422,976
AM Best Rating of A+ Or Higher	0.466	0.499	0.000	1.000
AM Best Rating of A	0.392	0.488	0.000	1.000
AM Best Rating of A-	0.142	0.349	0.000	1.000
Time indicators				
1995 indicator	0.216	0.412	0.000	1.000
1996 indicator	0.260	0.439	0.000	1.000
1997 indicator	0.253	0.435	0.000	1.000
1998 indicator	0.271	0.445	0.000	1.000

N = 66,426

In both states, the average **premium** (total premiums divided by insured house years) by policy form increases with the scope of coverage. This makes intuitive sense. Further, the average **price** varies by policy form.[3] The average price decreases as the scope of coverage increases. This is what one would expect as there are certain fixed expenses in servicing a given policy that would not increase as the underlying loss cost increases.

[3] We actually use PRICE1 = 1 + PRICE = [(1+r)(Premiums – ILC)]/[ILC] as our price variable; adding 1 to PRICE simply assures that our price measure in equation (3) is always positive.

Tables 5.3(a) and 5.3(b) provide the descriptive statistics for Florida and for New York based on the data used in our analysis. Note that average premiums and loss costs are higher in Florida than in New York. Also, as in Table 5.2, the measure of price (PRICE1 = Price + 1) is greater in New York than in Florida. In addition to the effect of fixed expenses (in relation to increasing loss costs), greater rate suppression and compression in Florida could contribute to its lower average price mark-up.

1. ESTIMATION OF QUANTITY DEMANDED

We estimate the model using the indicated loss costs (ILCs) (in the logged form) as our proxy of the quantity of insurance demanded. We also employed PRICE1 in the logged form as our proxy for price. PRICE1 is estimated as an endogenous variable, which is standard for demand models. We also account for several other endogenous variables including house value, deductibles, and the choice to invest in wind protection devices.

As noted above, the indicated loss costs in the PRICE equation were computed separately for each contract in our database. Since we wish to estimate the demand for catastrophe coverage as well as the demand for non-catastrophe coverage, we computed separately the catastrophe and non-catastrophe portions of indicated loss costs for each policy in the sample.[4] Thus, we can think of the homeowners' policy as a joint (or bundled) product where the coverage for the catastrophe peril and the coverage for non-catastrophe perils are typically but not always combined in the same contract. Further, consumers can vary or tradeoff the amounts of their catastrophe coverage and non-catastrophe coverage in their choice of coverage provisions (e.g., choosing higher wind deductibles). By estimating the two demands separately, we are acknowledging that different factors may affect the demands for insurance for these two sets of perils.

Before discussing the regression results in general, there are two sets of coefficients to highlight. The first is the price elasticity of demand. For Florida, the coefficient on the log of PRICE1 (Column 1 on Table 5.5) for the total demand equation is −1.079. This is almost unit elastic. However, if we decompose the price sensitivity of demand for catastrophe coverage,

---

[4] The decomposition of the non-catastrophe and catastrophe portions of indicated loss costs has become a standard feature of advisory loss cost filings and insurer pricing. The term "cat loading" is sometimes used to characterize the catastrophe component of the expected loss cost. Because catastrophes occur infrequently, modeling techniques must be used to calculate catastrophe loadings, as analysis of historical data is insufficient for this purpose. The cat expected loss costs used in this study were computed from the RMS catastrophe model in support of ISO loss cost estimations. While proprietary, interested readers can find more on the RMS model at http://www.rms.com/Catastrophe/Models/.

shown in Column 5, we see that it is even more elastic with an estimated coefficient of –1.915.[5] In contrast, the price elasticity for non-catastrophe coverage (Column 9) is approximately -0.40, which is inelastic. We see this same pattern in Table 5.6 for the New York results. However, in general, the demand for total insurance and its components is less price elastic in New York than in Florida.

While there have been relatively few demand studies for some insurance contracts, those that have been done have yielded elasticity estimates that vary widely. Table 5.4 provides estimated elasticities from other published studies for other lines of insurance. We note that our price elasticities are generally higher than those reported for other lines of insurance. In terms of income elasticity, our results seem to be in the same range as those reported by previous research. However, these results are not necessarily comparable, as none of the other studies, with the exception the individual health insurance study (Marquis and Long (1995)), use a relatively fully specified model with endogenously determined prices.

Table 5.4

Demand Elasticity Estimates

Price Elasticity	**Absolute Value of Elasticity**	**Citation**
Life	0.26 - 0.49	Babbel (1985)
Long Term Care	0.75 -1.25	Cohen and Weintrobe (2002)
Individual Health	0.17	Marquis and Long (1995)
Auto	0.57	Russell and Jaffee (1996)
Home		
Florida	1.08	Grace, Klein, Kleindorfer and Murray
New York	0.86	(See Tables 5.5-5.6 below)
National Flood Insurance	0.32	Brown and Hoyt (2000)
Crop Insurance	0.14 - 0.33	Barnett and Skees (1996)
Income Elasticity	**Actual Value of Elasticity**	
Life	0.006 - 0.008	Babbel (1985)
Long Term Care	None estimated	
Individual Health Insurance	0.15	Marquis and Long (1995)
Auto	0.16 - 1.71	Sherdan (1984)
Home		
Florida	.061	Grace, Klein, Kleindorfer and Murray
New York	-0.029	(See Tables 5.5-5.6 below)
National Flood Insurance	3.00	Brown and Hoyt (2000)
Crop Insurance	None estimated	

[5] Note here that the price elasticity measures for cat and non-cat are not defined in the traditional way. For example, since we only have a price variable for the total price (the price of cat and non-cat coverage bundled together), our elasticity is actually the percentage change in **total price** over the percentage change in the quantity demanded of cat coverage (or non-catastrophic cover).

Table 5.5 Two Stage Least Squares Results: Florida Contract Demand Equations For Total Loss Costs, Catastrophic Loss Costs, and Non-Catastrophic Loss Costs

	Variables	*Endogenous Variable*	Hypothesized sign	Total Indicated Lost Costs (1) Coefficient	(2) Std. Error	(3) t-stat	(4) Prob
1	Intercept		?	8.767	0.936	9.360	0.000
2	Selection Variable		?	0.018	0.021	0.880	0.379
	Insured Risk Characteristics						
1	Above Median For Both Cat And Non Cat Costs		+	0.308	0.011	28.590	0.000
2	Above Median For Cat And Below Median For Non Cat Costs		+	0.004	0.008	0.460	0.646
3	Above Median For Non Cat And Below Median For Cat Costs		+	0.002	0.005	0.490	0.624
4	% Of Homes With Frame Construction		+	0.225	0.027	8.210	0.000
5	% Of Homes With Brick Construction		+/-	0.119	0.028	4.310	0.000
6	Protection Code (1 is Highest)		+/-	0.037	0.001	32.460	0.000
	Contract Terms						
1	Log Of (Price +1)	x	-	-1.079	0.013	-80.070	0.000
2	% Of HO3 Policies In Zip Code		-	-0.205	0.010	-21.110	0.000
3	% Of HO8 Policies In Zip Code		-	0.314	0.101	3.120	0.002
4	% Of Policies With Wind Exclusion (FL Only)		-	0.330	0.026	12.510	0.000
5	% Of Policies With Replacement Cost Coverage		+	-0.001	0.008	-0.170	0.865
6	% Of Policies With Ord Or Law Coverage		+/-	0.101	0.018	5.480	0.000
7	Log Of Coverage A Limit		+	0.600	0.029	20.780	0.000
8	Log Of Wind Deductible	x	+/-	-0.015	0.009	-1.670	0.095
9	Log Of Fire Deductible	x	+/-	0.500	0.044	11.340	0.000
10	% With Wind Protection Device Credit (FL Only)	x	?	0.286	0.073	3.910	0.000
	Neighborhood Characteristics						
1	% Of Implemented Loss Costs To Indicated Loss Costs		-	-0.282	0.022	-12.590	0.000
2	Median Year Of Construction In Zip		-	-0.008	0.000	-30.450	0.000
3	% Of Homes In Zip Code With A Mortgage		+/-	-0.022	0.032	-0.690	0.490
4	Leverage Ratio Of Median Mortgage Costs To Median Income		?	6.022	0.566	10.640	0.000
5	Leverage Ratio Of Median Mortgage Costs To Median Home		?	-5.621	1.378	-4.080	0.000
6	Log Of Average Age Of Pop In Zip Code		?	0.025	0.036	0.700	0.484
7	% Of Households In Urban Areas		+/-	-0.013	0.006	-2.370	0.018
8	% Of Persons In Zip Aged 65 or Over		+	-0.366	0.053	-6.890	0.000
9	Log Of Median Income		+/-	0.061	0.019	3.250	0.001
	Neighborhood Characteristics						
1	Direct Writer		?	-0.961	0.119	-8.110	0.000
2	Stock Company		?	-0.571	0.172	-3.310	0.001
3	Log Of Auto Premiums Written By Company		?	0.017	0.003	6.590	0.000
4	Log Of Life Premiums Written By Associated Company		?	0.002	0.005	0.490	0.624
5	Log Of Total Assets Of Firm Selling Policy		?	0.332	0.040	8.330	0.000
6	Am Best Rating Of A		?	0.057	0.015	3.760	0.000
7	Am Best Rating Of A-		?	0.039	0.018	2.180	0.029
8	Am Best Rating Of B+		?	0.670	0.183	3.670	0.000
9	Am Best Rating Of Nr2		?	0.912	0.187	4.880	0.000
	Neighborhood Characteristics						
1	1996 Indicator		+	0.004	0.014	0.290	0.772
2	1997 Indicator		+	0.091	0.029	3.170	0.002
3	1998 Indicator		+	0.094	0.032	2.890	0.004
		N 40,971					
		R^2		0.937			

Table 5.5 Continued

	Catastrophic Indicated Loss Costs				Non-Catastrophic Indicated Loss Costs			
	(5)	(6)	(7)	(8)	(9)	(10)	(11)	(12)
	Coefficient	Std. Error	t-stat	Prob	Coefficient	Std. Error	t-stat	Prob
1	-6.797	3.229	-2.100	0.036	14.872	0.769	19.340	0.000
2	-0.628	0.072	-8.720	0.000	0.104	0.017	6.080	0.000
	Insured Risk Characteristics							
1	0.777	0.037	20.910	0.000	0.102	0.009	11.590	0.000
2	0.605	0.028	21.870	0.000	-0.261	0.007	-39.670	0.000
3	0.121	0.018	6.880	0.000	0.071	0.004	16.830	0.000
4	0.274	0.095	2.900	0.004	0.344	0.023	15.280	0.000
5	0.417	0.095	4.370	0.000	0.167	0.023	7.340	0.000
6	0.028	0.004	7.210	0.000	0.034	0.001	35.830	0.000
	Contract Terms							
1	-1.915	0.046	-41.210	0.000	-0.404	0.011	-36.490	0.000
2	-0.100	0.033	-2.990	0.003	-0.289	0.008	-36.230	0.000
3	0.069	0.347	0.200	0.841	0.145	0.083	1.750	0.080
4	0.292	0.091	3.210	0.001	0.400	0.022	18.430	0.000
5	-0.012	0.029	-0.410	0.682	0.098	0.007	14.110	0.000
6	-0.190	0.063	-3.000	0.003	0.149	0.015	9.900	0.000
7	-0.763	0.100	-7.660	0.000	0.784	0.024	33.050	0.000
8	0.114	0.031	3.640	0.000	-0.102	0.007	-13.640	0.000
9	2.670	0.152	17.580	0.000	-0.403	0.036	-11.160	0.000
10	-1.588	0.252	-6.310	0.000	0.540	0.060	9.010	0.000
	Neighborhood Characteristics							
1	-0.438	0.077	-5.660	0.000	-0.292	0.018	-15.870	0.000
2	-0.007	0.001	-7.340	0.000	-0.007	0.000	-34.610	0.000
3	0.540	0.110	4.920	0.000	-0.049	0.026	-1.870	0.061
4	13.777	1.952	7.060	0.000	4.881	0.465	10.500	0.000
5	-39.387	4.751	-8.290	0.000	-0.521	1.131	-0.460	0.646
6	0.643	0.124	5.170	0.000	-0.129	0.030	-4.360	0.000
7	0.092	0.019	4.720	0.000	-0.071	0.005	-15.370	0.000
8	-0.739	0.183	-4.030	0.000	-0.118	0.044	-2.700	0.007
9	0.315	0.065	4.860	0.000	0.105	0.015	6.780	0.000
	Neighborhood Characteristics							
1	-0.581	0.409	-1.420	0.156	-0.828	0.097	-8.510	0.000
2	-0.892	0.594	-1.500	0.134	-0.218	0.142	-1.540	0.124
3	0.018	0.009	2.040	0.041	0.020	0.002	9.410	0.000
4	0.121	0.018	6.880	0.000	0.071	0.004	16.830	0.000
5	0.238	0.138	1.730	0.084	0.206	0.033	6.280	0.000
6	0.625	0.052	11.970	0.000	-0.149	0.012	-11.980	0.000
7	0.493	0.062	8.010	0.000	-0.083	0.015	-5.660	0.000
8	0.285	0.629	0.450	0.653	0.310	0.150	2.070	0.038
9	0.705	0.644	1.100	0.271	0.435	0.153	2.830	0.005
	Neighborhood Characteristics							
1	0.199	0.048	4.150	0.000	0.003	0.011	0.250	0.803
2	0.355	0.099	3.570	0.000	0.096	0.024	4.050	0.000
3	0.452	0.112	4.030	0.000	0.077	0.027	2.880	0.004
	0.797				0.891			

Table 5.6 Two Stage Least Squares Results: New York Contract Demand Equations For Total Loss Costs, Catastrophic Loss Costs, and Non-Catastrophic Loss Costs

	Variables	*Endogenous Variable*	Hypothesized sign	Total Indicated Lost Costs (1) Coefficient	(2) Std. Error	(3) t-stat	(4) Prob
1	Intercept		?	0.817	0.336	2.430	0.015
2	Selection Variable		?	0.118	0.039	3.010	0.003
	Insured Risk Characteristics						
1	Above Median For Both Cat And Non Cat Costs			0.160	0.008	20.220	0.000
2	Above Median For Cat And Below Median For Non Cat Costs			-0.002	0.005	-0.320	0.749
3	Above Median For Non Cat And Below Median For Cat Costs			0.148	0.008	17.900	0.000
4	% Of Homes With Frame Construction		+	0.036	0.034	1.060	0.289
5	% Of Homes With Brick Construction		+/-	-0.020	0.035	-0.560	0.575
6	Protection Code (1 Is Highest)		+/-	0.035	0.001	33.340	0.000
	Contract Terms						
1	Log Of (Price +1)	x	-	-0.857	0.047	-18.380	0.000
2	% Of HO1 Policies In Zip Code (Ny Only)		-	0.003	0.032	0.110	0.912
3	% Of HO2 Policies In Zip Code (NY Only)		-	-0.163	0.020	-8.030	0.000
4	% Of HO3 Policies In Zip Code		-	-0.145	0.011	-13.650	0.000
5	% Of Policies With Replacement Cost Coverage		+	-0.023	0.008	-2.840	0.005
6	% Of Policies With Ord Or Law Coverage		+/-	0.028	0.005	5.110	0.000
7	Log Of Coverage A Limit	x	+	0.778	0.032	24.680	0.000
8	Log Of Wind Deductible	x	+/-	0.090	0.024	3.760	0.000
9	Log Of Fire Deductible	x	+/-	0.299	0.068	4.410	0.000
10	% Off Premises Coverage Exclusion (NY)		+	0.042	0.015	2.860	0.004
	Neighborhood Characteristics						
1	% Of Implemented Loss Costs To Indicated Loss Costs		-	-0.013	0.010	-1.340	0.180
2	Median Year Of Construction In Zip		-	-0.001	0.000	-6.090	0.000
3	% Of Homes In Zip Code With A Mortgage		+/-	-0.025	0.014	-1.770	0.077
4	Leverage Ratio Of Median Mortgage Costs To Median Income		?	-0.319	0.332	-0.960	0.337
5	Leverage Ratio Of Median Mortgage Costs To Median Home Value		?	-2.180	1.095	-1.990	0.047
6	Log Of Average Age Of Pop In Zip Code		?	-0.047	0.023	-2.030	0.042
7	% Of Households In Urban Areas		+/-	0.064	0.006	10.020	0.000
8	% Of Persons In Zip Aged 65 or Over		+	0.076	0.048	1.580	0.114
9	Log Of Median Income		+/-	-0.029	0.011	-2.630	0.009
	Firm Characteristics						
1	Direct Writer		?	-0.041	0.032	-1.280	0.201
2	Stock Company		?	0.059	0.021	2.760	0.006
3	Log Of Auto Premiums Written By Company		?	0.006	0.002	2.850	0.004
4	Log Of Life Premiums Written By Associated Company		?	0.020	0.002	12.140	0.000
5	Log Of Total Assets Of Firm Selling Policy		?	0.041	0.009	4.530	0.000
6	Am Best Rating Of A		?	0.012	0.006	1.940	0.052
7	Am Best Rating Of A-		?	0.040	0.009	4.570	0.000
	Time Indicators						
1	1996 Indicator		+	-0.006	0.003	-1.750	0.080
2	1997 Indicator		+	0.002	0.005	0.340	0.734
3	1998 Indicator		+	0.014	0.010	1.390	0.165
	N	66,426					
	R^2			0.819			

Table 5.6 Continued

	Catastrophic Indicated Loss Costs				Non-Catastrophic Indicated Loss Costs			
	(5)	(6)	(7)	(8)	(9)	(10)	(11)	(12)
	Coefficie	Std. Error	t-stat	Prob	Coefficien	Std. Error	t-stat	Prob
1	-13.553	0.796	-17.030	0.000	0.823	0.454	1.810	0.070
2	-0.308	0.093	-3.330	0.001	0.257	0.053	4.860	0.000
	Insured Risk Characteristics							
1	0.751	0.019	40.110	0.000	0.102	0.011	9.520	0.000
2	0.648	0.012	53.070	0.000	-0.025	0.007	-3.570	0.000
3	-0.315	0.020	-16.070	0.000	0.109	0.011	9.690	0.000
4	0.654	0.080	8.150	0.000	-0.114	0.046	-2.480	0.013
5	-0.360	0.079	-4.540	0.000	-0.044	0.038	-1.170	0.242
6	-0.011	0.002	-4.290	0.000	0.039	0.001	27.360	0.000
	Contract Terms							
1	-2.064	0.110	-18.720	0.000	-0.331	0.063	-5.260	0.000
2	0.233	0.075	3.120	0.002	-0.055	0.043	-1.300	0.194
3	0.564	0.048	11.710	0.000	-0.320	0.027	-11.630	0.000
4	0.261	0.025	10.420	0.000	-0.237	0.014	-16.580	0.000
5	0.049	0.019	2.530	0.011	-0.024	0.011	-2.140	0.032
6	0.038	0.013	2.930	0.003	0.024	0.007	3.240	0.001
7	1.231	0.075	16.490	0.000	0.594	0.043	13.940	0.000
8	0.423	0.057	7.440	0.000	-0.037	0.032	-1.150	0.250
9	-1.124	0.161	-7.000	0.000	0.780	0.092	8.510	0.000
10	0.345	0.035	9.970	0.000	-0.068	0.020	-3.440	0.001
	Neighborhood Characteristics							
1	-0.074	0.023	-3.160	0.002	-0.019	0.013	-1.410	0.159
2	0.003	0.000	10.570	0.000	-0.001	0.000	-4.100	0.000
3	0.218	0.033	6.550	0.000	-0.043	0.019	-2.260	0.024
4	0.452	0.784	0.580	0.562	-2.336	0.448	-5.210	0.000
5	-16.632	2.590	-6.420	0.000	6.278	1.479	4.250	0.000
6	0.151	0.055	2.740	0.006	-0.122	0.031	-3.870	0.000
7	-0.069	0.015	-4.570	0.000	0.094	0.009	10.950	0.000
8	0.953	0.113	8.420	0.000	0.005	0.065	0.080	0.936
9	0.248	0.026	9.590	0.000	-0.038	0.015	-2.570	0.010
	Firm Characteristics							
1	-0.334	0.075	-4.430	0.000	0.066	0.043	1.540	0.124
2	0.469	0.050	9.310	0.000	-0.097	0.029	-3.370	0.001
3	0.005	0.005	0.860	0.390	0.006	0.003	2.130	0.033
4	0.014	0.004	3.750	0.000	0.021	0.002	9.350	0.000
5	0.114	0.021	5.390	0.000	0.012	0.012	0.990	0.322
6	-0.048	0.011	-4.140	0.000	-0.016	0.005	-2.980	0.003
7	0.007	0.018	0.390	0.697	-0.015	0.009	-1.730	0.084
	Time Indicators							
1	0.020	0.007	2.660	0.008	-0.016	0.004	-3.670	0.000
2	0.120	0.013	9.270	0.000	-0.045	0.007	-6.050	0.000
3	0.278	0.024	11.530	0.000	-0.090	0.014	-6.500	0.000
	0.691				0.731			

As with any incomplete set of panel data, there is a need to address up front the potential for possible selection bias. In particular, are the companies in our database (all ISO respondents) representative of all insurers selling homeowners insurance in Florida and New York. In our sample, we have 60 companies in the sample over the four years. In Florida, this represents about 30 percent of the total homeowners' premiums written in each year. In New York, our sample companies write about 35 percent of the market. The firms in our sample may be significantly different than the other firms in the market. We control for this probability by estimating a probit regression that attempts to classify those companies that are in our sample, i.e., they are companies that report data to ISO and not other statistical agents.[6] This selection model employs firm specific characteristics to determine whether the firm is an "ISO Reporter."[7]

From this regression, we obtain the inverse Mills ratio for each observation as $\lambda = -\phi(X'\beta)/\Phi(X'\beta)$ from the estimates of the probit regression where $\varphi(*)$ represents the normal density function and $\Phi(*)$ represents the cumulative normal distribution function (see Green, 2000). This variable can be employed in the demand equation to account for the fact that only some firms report to ISO. In our model, the coefficient on λ in the demand equation represents the effect on the quantity demanded for a firm that reports data to ISO. If the coefficient is positive (negative), then the mean level of demand is higher (lower) relative to firms who do not report to ISO, all other things being equal.

For our Florida results, in Table 5.5, the selection indicator (λ) is significantly negative for catastrophe coverage, thus implying that consumers are less likely to demand catastrophe coverage from ISO reporting companies than from non-ISO reporting companies.[8] However, our selection indicator is significantly positive for non-catastrophe, implying that consumers are more likely to demand non-catastrophe coverage from ISO

---

6 In Florida and New York, regulators require insurers to report statistical data to one of several designated statistical agents. ISO and the National Association of Independent Insurers (NAII) are the two principal statistical agents; other statistical agents account for only a small portion of insurers operating in these markets. An increasing number of insurers have selected ISO as their statistical agent, which has broadened the types of insurers in its database. At the same time, among the ISO reporting firms, several declined to authorize the use of their data for this study. These tended to be insurers with more unique products and portfolios of exposures.

7 The regression we estimate is: *Probit* [(ISO Reporter and Participant) =1, 0 otherwise] = *f*(log of total assets, log of Florida homeowners premiums, Best Capital Adequacy Ratio, business concentration ratio (top four lines), geographical four state concentration ratio, percent of claims paid within two years, percent of claim value paid within two years, Stock Dummy, Direct Writer Dummy, and year dummies).

8 Several large "direct writers" with significant amounts of exposures in coastal areas report their statistical data to NAII.

reporting companies. Overall, we see that the selection indicator is not significantly different from zero. Thus, the opposing effects of selection are netted-out in the overall demand for homeowners insurance in Florida. In Table 5.6, we see the same results for New York - the selection parameter is negative for catastrophe demand and positive for non-catastrophe coverage catastrophe and non-catastrophe coverage combined. For the overall level of demand for catastrophe and non-catastrophe coverage combined, the coefficient for our selection variable takes a positive sign for both Florida and New York, but is only significant for New York

2. FLORIDA RESULTS

2.1 Insured Risk Characteristics

First we construct variables based upon the standard base loss costs for a particular type of home with a given set of coverages in a Zip code. This standard base loss cost is employed to provide an index for the level of risk in the Zip code. We calculate four indicator variables based on the standard loss costs based on whether the Zip code is above (or below) the median standard loss costs for cat loss costs or non-cat loss costs. Thus, we have HH (above median for both cat and non-cat standard costs), HL and LH (above median for one, but not the other) and LL (below median for both cat and non-cat standard loss costs). In Florida the HH Zip codes are in South Florida and in the Tampa-St. Petersburg-Clearwater area. In contrast the LL area is north and central Florida.

We hypothesize higher risk areas are likely to have higher demand for coverage, all other things being equal. We see this is true for those Zip codes that have above median costs for both cat and non-cat risks. The HL and LH indicator variables are not significant for overall demand. However, we see that all three "risk" variables are significantly related to the demand for catastrophic coverage. In contrast, for non-catastrophic coverage all three are significant, but the HL (above median for cat and below median for non-cat) is negatively related to the demand for coverage.

In estimating the effect of the construction type, superior fire resistant homes (SFR) are treated as the base case in our specification of dummy variables (i.e., SFR is omitted to avoid multicollinearity with indicators for other construction types). *A priori*, one would expect demand to be lower for the SFR homes if fire risk was a major component of the demand for insurance. Thus, we would hypothesize consumers with wooden frame homes would have a higher demand for insurance than consumers with SFR homes. Our results support this hypothesis. Further, this relationship is strong and significant for both catastrophe and non-catastrophe coverage.

For brick construction, we see a positive and significant relationship for the overall demand and for demand both catastrophe and non-catastrophe coverage. This suggests that, relative to owners of SFR homes, owners of brick homes tend to have a higher demand for insurance.

The protection code is the ISO-designated rating of the local community's fire and police protection. A higher code means the protection level is lower and implies that risk is higher. Consistent with this, we see in our statistical results that as the protection code increases (public services are of lower quality), the demand for insurance increases.

2.2 Contract Terms

In addition to price, there are a number of other variables that reflect various contract choices. The first is policy type. Recall that the HO5 policy offers the broadest coverage (omitted to avoid multicollinearity) and should be the most preferred, all other things equal including price. If HO5 polices are preferred to all other policies, then there should be negative coefficients on the percentages of HO3 and HO8 polices in a Zip code. Our results are partially consistent with this hypothesis as the percentage of HO3 policies in a Zip is negatively related to the demand for coverage. This is true across the various types of coverage: catastrophe, non-catastrophe and combined. However, our estimations yield a positive coefficient for the percentage of HO8 policies in the total demand equation; One explanation for this result is that HO8 policies tend to be written in older urban neighborhoods where the risk of non-catastrophe perils such as fire and theft can be very high.

In Florida, insureds can elect to have coverage for windstorms excluded from their policy (presuming they are not prevented from doing so by a lender's insurance requirements). We would expect that a wind exclusion would negatively affect demand. However, our results yield a positive coefficient for this variable suggesting that it has a positive effect on demand. This is true for both the catastrophe coverage and non-catastrophe coverage equations and may be due to the fact that the Zips with a high percentage of excluded polices are in higher risk Zip codes where the Florida wind pool was providing low cost coverage against windstorms. The availability of low cost protection against hurricanes may have increased demand for insurance overall.

If consumers value policy options such as replacement cost coverage on contents, then the addition of these options should be associated with higher levels of demand if the benefits of the options outweigh their incremental cost to consumers. For replacement cost coverage, we see this is true only for non-catastrophe coverage. The regression coefficient on replacement cost coverage is not significant for overall demand or for catastrophe coverage, which implies that consumers do not value it in excess of its cost. These findings suggest that being able to replace property damaged from fire or loss through theft may be of significant concern to homeowners, whereas repairing structural damage may be the principal concern with respect to the wind peril.[9]

Ordinance or law coverage increases demand for both non-catastrophe coverage and overall coverage. Ordinance or law coverage is a policy option that will pay the additional costs of repairing a home to the standards of any new ordinances or building codes that have been instituted since the home was built. This is not surprising as Florida has significantly strengthened its building codes since Hurricane Andrew occurred, increasing the value of this additional coverage for homeowners. However, we see that ordinance or law coverage is not valued for the catastrophe coverage.

A further issue is that the demand for homeowners insurance is actually a derived demand from the demand for housing. We account for the demand for housing by including the value of the insurance contract's Coverage A limit, which reflects the value of the individual's house as an endogenous variable. Factors expected to influence housing demand include such Zip code characteristics as median income and Census reported housing characteristics, and these factors are used as instrumental variables in our two-stage least squares estimation below.

The Coverage A limit (on the dwelling and attached structures) is our proxy for the replacement cost of the home and is treated as an endogenous variable.[10] One would expect that insurance demand would increase as the replacement cost of the home increases, all other things held constant. Our results are generally consistent with this expectation. As the value of the home (Coverage A limit) increases, the quantity of insurance demanded increases. An interesting exception is for catastrophe coverage. In this case, we see that demand does not rise with housing values, perhaps because the incremental cost of additional coverage exceeds its perceived utility.

The fire and wind deductibles are also endogenously determined. Higher deductibles may increase or decrease the demand for insurance. First, as the deductible increases, the premium should fall reflecting the lower loss costs

---

9 Indeed, in areas with a high catastrophe risk (and high catastrophe loadings in the coast of insurance), insureds may forgo replacement cost coverage on personal property in order to afford and purchase more adequate structural coverage for catastrophe losses.

10 As mentioned earlier, insurers typically require a homeowner to carry a Coverage A limit equal to at least 70 80 percent of the replacement cost of his home. Limits on the other property coverages are stated as percentages of the Coverage A limit. Further, the problem of inadequate coverage limits has received increasing attention and has probably prompted insureds and insurers to maintain coverage limits closer to the replacement cost of homes.

covered by the policy. Whether the price falls or not depends on the ratio of premium reductions to loss cost reductions (see equation (3). In any case, the homeowner may use the premium savings to purchase additional coverages that are considered to be a better "value", such as higher policy limits. Indeed, insurance experts commonly advise trading higher deductibles for higher limits.[11] In addition, as the deductible increases, the value of the coverage decreases and the consumer bears more risk. Demand for the resulting lower-valued coverage could also decrease. Thus, the sign of the deductible's coefficient gives us some indication which effect is more important: the premium-reduction effect or the coverage effect.

For overall demand, we see that the coefficient for the wind deductible is negative but just barley significant at the 10% level. This implies that the coverage effect dominates. Increases in deductibles reduce the demand for insurance, all other things held constant. However, if we look at the coefficient in Column 5, we see that it is positive and quite significant, implying consumers value a higher wind deductible for catastrophe coverage because the premium-reduction effect dominates. Higher deductibles imply lower premiums, and this encourages consumers to purchase more insurance. This is plausible as consumers facing greater catastrophe risk may be more concerned about having adequate coverage to cover large losses than absorbing a larger deductible in the event of a hurricane.[12] For the non-catastrophe coverage equation, the wind deductible is negative indicating that the coverage effect dominates. This is also plausible, as non-catastrophe perils tend to involve more frequent and smaller losses not related to wind.

For the fire deductible, we see a different phenomenon. The coefficient on the fire deductible in the total demand equation is positive, implying that the increase in the deductible lowers premium sufficiently to increase demand. For catastrophe coverage, the relationship is also positive and significant. Catastrophes (hurricanes) are not fire related,, and thus higher fire deductible's effect on premium leaves more funds available to purchase other coverage. However, in Column 9, we see that, for non-catastrophe coverage, the coefficient on the fire deductible is negative, suggesting that coverage effect dominates the premium-reduction effect in the demand for non-catastrophe coverage.

Finally, we treat the decision to employ a windstorm protection device such as storm shutters as endogenous. There is no *a priori* hypothesis

---

[11] The expense load and price mark-up on lower deductibles are very high. Insureds likely become increasingly attuned to this as their premium increases, as revealed by a significant increase in the size of the deductibles chosen by policyholders in Florida and New York discussed in Chapter 2.

[12] We should note it is likely that insurers have made the pricing of large deductibles very attractive to consumers as this viewed as one of several effective strategies to manage an insurer's catastrophe exposure.

regarding the effect of this variable on the overall demand for insurance but the presence of such devices could lead to increases in demand for non-catastrophe insurance. If the presence of protection devices increases demand for insurance, then the protection devices are complements to traditional insurance. In contrast, if there is a negative relationship between the presence of the protection devices and insurance demand, then one might reasonably conclude that the devices were a substitute for traditional insurance. Our coefficient results are positive for overall and non-cat coverage, implying that the windstorm device credit is associated with higher insurance demand, all other things held constant. However, we see that negative effect for the cat demand suggesting that the device is a potential substitute for insurance.

2.3 Neighborhood Characteristics and Regulation

The first neighborhood characteristic is the ratio of implemented loss costs to indicated loss costs. This also may be viewed as a regulatory variable as regulators tend to vary the severity of price constraints by rating territory. Because regulators seek to keep insurance "affordable", their constraints are more severe or binding in higher-cost areas. The implemented loss costs are those costs that the regulator allows to be used in making full rate calculations for homeowners' policies in a given rating territory. As mentioned previously, we think of this ratio as a measurement of rate suppression or rate compression.[13] As the implemented loss costs are reduced by regulation (relative to the expected or indicated loss costs), the consumer gets a lower price for coverage. As the ratio increases, the price reduction diminishes. Thus one would expect that a higher ratio would reduce the demand for coverage. As regulatory price suppression is reduced, price rises, and as price rises, the quantity demanded falls. In fact, we find this to be the case for all three demand functions.

Older homes tend to be higher risk and one would expect that their owners would have a higher demand for coverage, all other things equal. Our results are consistent with this - as the median year of a home's construction in a Zip code increases (i.e., it is a newer home), the demand for coverage falls. This is true for all three Florida demand models.

---

[13] We define "rate suppression" as a binding regulatory ceiling on the overall rate level charged by an insurer. "Rate compression" is defined as a binding regulatory constraint on the rate differential between low and high-risk territories. In practice, regulators tend to both compress and suppress rates by imposing severe constraints on the rates for the highest-risk territories, without a compensating increase in the rates for low-risk territories to produce an adequate overall rate level.

The percentage of homes with a mortgage may have either a positive or a negative effect on demand. Mortgage lenders generally require homeowners insurance to complete the mortgage transaction. This implies that the greater the percentage of homes with mortgages, the greater the demand for insurance. However, while borrowers must meet certain insurance coverage requirements, they are not required to purchase the broadest coverage available. Further, consumers may scrimp on their insurance if they have low equity (which could also increase their mortgage payments). This moral hazard phenomenon may result in a negative coefficient on the percentage of homes in a Zip code with a mortgage. Another reason that the percentage of homes with a mortgage may be related to the demand for insurance may involve an owner's tenure in a home. Mortgages are paid off over time, but consumers do not necessarily update their insurance coverage each year.[14] Thus, in Zip codes with a higher percentage of mortgages, it may be that the case that people have shorter tenure in their homes and that their insurance is more up to date. On the other hand, the lower the percentage of homes with mortgages, the higher people's equity in their homes may be, potentially increasing their demand for insurance , everything else held constant.

We see that, in Florida, the percentage of mortgages in a Zip code is negatively related to the total demand for insurance. This relationship is positive for catastrophe coverage but negative for non-catastrophe coverage. This suggests that, for non-catastrophe coverage, the moral hazard explanation and/or "equity effect" dominates the decision to purchase insurance. However, it is interesting to see that as the percentage of mortgages increases in a Zip code, the demand for catastrophe coverage increases. It is not clear why the moral hazard effect and/or the equity effect should be that different between the demands for catastrophe and non-catastrophe coverages. One possibility is that lenders impose greater insurance requirements or insurers are more diligent in updating coverage limits for homes subject to greater catastrophe risk.

We further examine the relationship between housing costs, homeowner equity (or leverage) and the demand for insurance with additional variables. The first such variable is the ratio of median housing costs for homes with mortgages (in the Zip code) to the median income in the Zip. Housing costs include mortgage expenditures, taxes, insurance, and fuel costs. The higher the ratio of housing costs to income, the tighter is a homeowner's budget constraint for non-housing expenditures. A positive relationship between this ratio and demand would imply that, while cash poor, the homeowner wishes to avoid default on his mortgage (due to uninsured losses) and thus will

---

[14] Some insurers and agents may not periodically review their insureds' coverage limits for adequacy. The replacement cost of a home can increase due to improvements by the homeowner, as well as general inflation in building costs.

purchase more insurance. A negative coefficient would imply that consumers attempt to scrimp on their insurance coverage as they have less money to spend on non-housing items. Our results yield a positive coefficient for the housing cost/income ratio in all three demand functions. This suggests that homeowners' aversion to risk and default dominates over concerns about having to economize on non-housing items. We should also note that high housing costs relative to income may reflect the importance of housing to a consumer, and this could also increase the demand for insurance. Further, Florida law protects a person's entire home value from a bankruptcy proceeding. Thus, as long as a person can pay their mortgage, one cannot lose a home though bankruptcy. Other states like New York protect a much smaller amount ($10,000).

A second variable is the ratio of mortgage costs to the median home value. This is a measure of a homeowner's leverage, i.e., higher mortgage payments relative to home value imply less equity. As leverage increases, one would expect a reduced incentive to purchase insurance. In Florida, we see that the coefficient on this ratio is negative in all three demand equations and significant in two (total demand and catastrophe demand.) This suggests that as the ratio of mortgage costs to home value increases (i.e., leverage increases), the demand for insurance decreases.

A plausible story emerges from these results. Cash-strapped homeowners who place a high value on their housing may be primarily concerned with avoiding uninsured losses and negative credit ratings that would arise from default on their mortgage or other debts. On the other hand, all other things equal, highly leveraged homeowners (rich or poor), may be inclined to take their chances on incurring uninsured losses from a low-probability event that could force them to default on their mortgage.

There is no *a priori* expectation on the sign of the coefficient for the average age of the population in a Zip code. On the one hand, families with young children may tend to be more risk averse and have a higher demand for insurance. On the other hand, young single homeowners may be less risk averse than older homeowners. Other factors associated with age and risk aversion may confound the relationship between age and the demand for insurance we observe. Some elderly homeowners may be very risk averse, while others may be less concerned about the risk of financial losses because they have a shorter time horizon or greater assets. In our results, we see that the coefficient for the age variable is not significant in the equation for overall demand. However, age has a significant and positive effect on the demand for catastrophe insurance. This implies that, while the overall effect of age is not significant, age does positively influence the demand for catastrophe insurance. This may be because, as consumers age, they have greater equity in their homes and have more to loose in a catastrophe.

However, we see that age is negatively related to demand for non-catastrophe insurance, which implies that older consumers demand less non-cat coverage. If age is related to wealth, then older consumers may feel they have the resources to cover most non-catastrophe losses but be concerned about their ability to withstand infrequent but large catastrophe losses , all else being equal. Younger consumers may be more concerned about their ability to withstand more frequent but smaller non-catastrophe losses.

Since Florida is a retirement state, it is appropriate to look at the effect that the percentage of retirees may have on the demand for insurance. We proxy retirees in the Zip code by the number of people 65 years old or older. If we look at the total demand equation, we see a negative relationship between retirees and the demand for insurance. This relationship is also found in the catastrophic and non-catastrophic demand. This does suggest a shorter time horizon and a corresponding reduction in value of insurance.

The percentage of households in urban areas should be related to insurance demand. This is because of greater risk of fire spreading to a home from an adjacent property, higher crime rates in urban areas, and because urban homes tend to have higher exposure to catastrophe risk (to the extent that urban areas are concentrated along the nation's coasts). Note that the coastal areas in Florida tend to have the highest population concentrations because of their attractiveness to retirees, tourists and others. (Note: deleted the stuff about home values because we control for that.) If they are higher risk, then the relationship may be positive. We see that in Florida, the percentage of urban households is negatively related to overall demand and demand for non-catastrophe coverage, , suggesting that the people who live in urban areas are generally less risk averse than others, all else being equal. But the percentage of urban households is positively related to demand for catastrophe insurance, suggesting that the urban-catastrophe risk association dominates in the demand for catastrophe coverage.

Finally, we examine income. The expected sign on, and the magnitude of, the coefficient for income is ambiguous because of two competing hypotheses. First, insurance may be thought of as an inferior good. If the coefficient on income is negative, it implies that increases in income reduce the demand for insurance. Arrow (1971) conjectured that individuals have declining absolute risk aversion. This implies that, as income increases, the demand for insurance should diminish. Mossin (1968), in turn, proved that if a person faced a price of insurance greater than the actuarially fair value, but below the price at which no insurance would be purchased, and the consumer exhibited decreasing absolute risk aversion, then the amount of insurance coverage fell as wealth increased. Mossin did not consider the case where higher incomes might generate more assets at risk and thus the higher income person would have greater losses to insure against. This yields the alternative hypothesis that income could have a positive coefficient in the insurance demand equation.

Further, Briys, Dionne and Eeckhoudt (1989) have pointed out that the income demand elasticity for insurance will be positive if and only if absolute risk aversion does not decrease significantly rapidly enough or, if and only if the variation of risk aversion is lower than a minimal bound. Cleeton and Zellner (1993) undertake a similar analysis and operationalize Briys et al.'s conclusion slightly differently. They find that the income elasticity of demand for insurance will be positive over all prices if $\varphi_a + \eta > 1$ where φ_a is the elasticity of relative risk aversion to initial income and η is the elasticity of the amount at risk with respect to initial income. This implies that if potential losses change as wealth changes (which makes sense in this analysis as wealthier people may buy more expensive houses, exposing themselves to higher potential losses), we may see a positive relationship between income and insurance purchased.

Our estimated coefficients on income are positive, but relatively inelastic. This implies one of two things. First, while we control for housing value, we may not be capturing all of the relationships between higher income and higher demand for housing. Alternatively, the positive relationship can be due to the decreasing effect on the demand for insurance due to decreasing absolute risk aversion.[15]

If we look at Table 5.4 above, we see that most insurance demand studies obtain relatively low demand estimates. Our results are consistent with most of the reported income elasticities.

2.4 Firm Characteristics

In Florida, consumers tend to buy coverage from agency writers and mutual companies. For all three demand equations, there is a negative relationship between the demand for insurance and being a direct a writer, although it is not significant in the case of catastrophe insurance. Similarly, for all three demand equations, there is a negative relationship between demand for insurance and being a stock company, although it is only significant in the equation for overall demand. We included auto premiums written by the insured's homeowners carrier to account for some potential consumer transactions cost savings from dealing with one insurer and

[15] We estimated a regression between the log of the median home value and the log of income holding other things constant such as the characteristics of the house, insurance prices, and neighborhood characteristics constant. The elasticity of median house value with respect to income, our measure of η, was estimated to be 1.04. Thus, as long as φ_a was greater than (approximately) -.04 we would expect to see a positive elasticity between income and the amount of insurance purchased.

discounts for buying multiple policies from the same provider. We find that the coefficient on auto premiums is positive, which implies that consumers value being able to purchase homeowners insurance and auto insurance from the same carrier. Further, we see a significantly positive relationship for life premiums written by a sister company and the demand for catastrophe insurance and the demand for non-catastrophe insurance. Again, we conjecture that consumers like the ability to deal with one insurance company. There is also a positive relationship between life premiums and overall demand for homeowners insurance, but it is not significant.

The size of the company is also a proxy for its soundness, reputation and/or its ability to achieve economies of scale. Our conjecture here is that larger companies are perceived to be financially stronger and are able to take advantage of economies of scale. For our sample companies, company size has a positive effect on all three demands.[16]

Another indication of firm solvency quality is its A.M. Best Rating of its claims paying ability. In this model, the A+ and higher category is the omitted category. If a high rating is valuable, then each of the other rating coefficients should be negative. If consumers favor lower prices over greater financial strength, then we might see negative coefficients on all of the higher ratings and a positive coefficient on the lower ratings.

In fact, we see in Table 5.5 that the coefficients for companies with ratings lower than the omitted category are generally positive and significant, paradoxically suggesting that consumers prefer to purchase insurance from companies that are less financially secure. [17] One interpretation of this perverse result is that insurers' Best ratings are correlated with other factors omitted from this analysis. We also note that, while guaranty fund coverage is not widely publicized, consumers may know that they will receive some protection in case of an insurer's insolvency, which would lessen the value they place on financial strength. The moral hazard effects of guaranty fund coverage have received considerable attention in the insurance economics literature (see Cummins, 1988 for example) and we explore this further in the last part of our analysis.

---

[16] It is interesting to note that the 12 insurers that became insolvent because of Hurricane Andrew were relatively small companies.

[17] The company with a NR2 rating appears to be an anomaly. Category NR2 is a not rated category. One firm is in the date set with an NR2 rating. The reason the firm was not rated is because company started operation right after Hurricane Andrew, thus A.M. Best did not have the ability to properly rate the company. This firm is a wholly owned subsidiary of an A++ rated company. Thus, the company is not exactly a high-risk firm. Currently, it holds an A rating from A.M. Best. In light of these facts, if we look at the catastrophe demand, we see that consumers value a strong company, but not necessarily the strongest company.

3. NEW YORK

We also estimated demand equations for New York to see how different market and regulatory conditions affect our findings. Coastal areas of New York, such as Long Island, face a moderate degree of catastrophe risk. Regulatory constraints on insurers' rates appear to have been less severe in New York because cost pressures have been more moderate. We would not expect the risk of non-catastrophe perils in urban areas to be eclipsed by catastrophe risk as in Florida. We employ similar demand models in our analysis of the New York market, with some adjustments to reflect coverage options specific to New York.

3.1 Insured Risk Characteristics

For New York in Table 5.6, we see some differences compared to the results we obtained for Florida after controlling for selection bias and whether the zip code is an area with above median cat and non-catastrophic losses. Relative to superior fire resistant (SFR) structures, owners of brick homes have a lower demand for insurance, but the effect is only significant for catastrophe insurance. We also see that, while owners of wood frame homes have a significantly higher demand for catastrophe coverage, they have a significantly lower demand for non-catastrophe insurance. The reason for the negative effect of brick and frame homes (relative to SFR homes) is not immediately obvious – it is possible that owners of SFR homes are more risk averse and purchase more insurance as well as make other investments to lower risk. Further, as in Florida, as the quality of public protection services declines (that is, as public protection grades rise from best to worst), the demand for overall coverage and non-catastrophe coverage increases. It is interesting to note that the demand for catastrophe coverage is negatively related to the quality of public protection services. That is, as the as public protection grades rise, there is reduction in the quantity of catastrophe insurance demand.

We also undertake to examine the ILCs above and below the median. Thus, we have HH (above median for both cat and not-cat standard costs), HL and LH (Above median for one, but not the other) and LL (below median for both cat and not cat standard loss costs). In New York, the HH area is Long Island, while the LL area is most of the remainder of New York State and again serves as the omitted category. As is the case with our results for Florida, being in an HH location has a significantly positive effect in all three demand equations. Our results for LH and HL locations are somewhat ambiguous.

3.2 Contract Terms

If we examine the policy choices in New York in Table 5.6, we see that HO2 and HO3 policies have negative coefficients for overall and non-catastrophe demand, implying that they are not valued as highly as HO5 polices, which is the omitted category. In turn, HO2 and HO3 policies have positive coefficients in the demand for catastrophe coverage. These findings likely reflect the fact that HO 2 and HO3 policies provide less protection against non-catastrophe losses than HO5 policies but similar protection against catastrophe losses. Further we see that HO1 policies are preferred to HO5 policies for overall coverage and catastrophe coverage but not non-catastrophe coverage, perhaps because of the limited protection that HO1 policies provide against non-catastrophe perils.

Replacement cost coverage on personal property has a negative sign for total demand. This suggests that the average consumer does not value this option. If we look at cat demand, we see that replacement cost coverage is positive and is valued by the average consumer. However, for non-cat cover, it is again negative.

Ordinance or law coverage has positive signs for all coverages, suggesting that the average consumer does value this additional policy option, all else being equal. We should note that the problem of substandard construction and the need to strengthen building codes have not been issues in New York, unlike the case in Florida. Thus, including ordinance or law coverage probably does not add as much to the overall cost of coverage as it does in Florida.

As in Florida, we see that the Coverage A limit is positively related to overall demand and demand for non-catastrophe insurance in New York. However, unlike Florida, we see that Coverage A limit is also positively related to demand for catastrophe insurance in New York. Thus, the higher value of the home as measured by the coverage A limit, the more insurance is demanded by New York consumers.

As is the case for Florida, the coefficients on the wind deductible is positive for catastrophe insurance but negative for non-catastrophe insurance (albeit insignificant in New York). Unlike Florida, the coefficient for wind deductibles in the equation for overall demand is positive in New York.

Also as the case in Florida, the coefficients for fire deductibles for New York are generally positive. In New York, however, the coefficient for the fire deductible is negative in the equation for catastrophe insurance, whereas in Florida, it is negative in the equation for non-catastrophe demand.

Nonetheless, it is generally the case in New York that, as wind and fire deductibles rise, consumers purchase more insurance. That increases in wind deductibles are associated with increases in demand for catastrophe insurance suggests that consumers use their savings from higher wind deductibles to purchase additional protection against catastrophes, while the positive relationship between fire deductibles and demand for non-catastrophe insurance suggests that consumers use the savings from higher fire deductibles to buy additional protection against non-catastrophe losses.

Finally, New York also allows homeowners policies to exclude off-premises theft coverage. This exclusion should reduce the price of insurance. One would expect a positive effect on demand for this exclusion if consumers preferred the exclusion given the resulting premium discount (or alternatively did not value the coverage enough to pay the higher cost). What we see is that the coefficient on the exclusion variable has a positive sign except in the equation for non-catastrophe demand, implying that consumers opting for the exclusion purchase more insurance, all other things equal. This makes sense as it suggests that consumers who exclude off premises losses can use the premium savings to expand other coverages

3.3 Neighborhood Characteristics and Regulation

Looking at the regulatory subsidy variable - the ratio of the implemented loss costs to the indicated loss costs (our measure of price suppression/compression) - we generally obtain the same results we obtained in Florida. That is, as the ratio increased, prices were allowed to rise closer to their market level and the demand for insurance decreased. Recall that rate suppression and compression in Florida was much more severe than in New York. Note that, for a given ratio, the amount of the subsidy in Florida would be higher because loss costs and premiums are considerably higher in Florida. This could explain why, for New York, the subsidy effect is insignificant in the equations for total demand and non-catastrophe demand.

The median year of construction is expected to be negatively related to the demand for insurance. In our regression results, the coefficient for year of construction is negative and statistically significant in the equations for total demand and demand for non-catastrophe insurance. But, for catastrophe demand, the relationship is positive and significant, but small in magnitude. This could be caused by greater new home construction in coastal areas.

The percentage of homes with mortgages has a significantly positive effect on demand for catastrophe insurance but has significantly negative effects on demand for non-catastrophe insurance and demand overall. As we suggest for Florida, lenders may impose more stringent insurance requirements in areas subject to coastal windstorms.

The pattern for the measures related to housing costs and leverage (the ratio of mortgages costs to income and the ratio of mortgage costs to home value, respectively) exhibit a different pattern than in Florida. The measure of the tightness of the budget constraint is not statistically significant in either the total or catastrophe demand equation. However, the coefficient for this variable is significantly negative in the non-catastrophe demand equation. This implies that, as their budgets become tighter, consumers demand less insurance for perils other than catastrophes, all other things held constant. For the leverage ratio, the estimated coefficient is negative and significant in the total and catastrophic demand equations, as was the case with our results for Florida. But the coefficient for this variable is significantly positive in the non-catastrophe demand equations, which differs from our results for Florida. It is possible that the high price of land in certain areas of New York counteracts any moral hazard effect associated with higher leverage.[18]

Age appears to affect all three demands for coverage. Age is negatively related to total demand and for non-cat demand, but is positive and significant for catastrophic demand. This contrasts with what we found for Florida. Also, the percentage of people over age 65 affects demand differently in New York than in Florida. The coefficient for this variable in all three demand equations, but it is significant only in the equation for the catastrophe insurance. It is possible that elderly homeowners in more catastrophe-prone areas in New York have greater reason to secure their homes for themselves and their heirs.

In addition, the percentage of homes in urban areas is positively related to overall demand and the demand for non-catastrophe coverage, reflecting the increased risk level of urban homes. However, in the demand for catastrophe coverage, the relationship between percentage of homes urban areas and demand is negative.

Finally, we see that in New York, insurance is generally an inferior good. As income increases, the demand for total coverage and non-catastrophe coverage decreases. In contrast, increases in income are associated with increases the demand for catastrophe coverage.

3.4 Firm Characteristics

In New York, the type of distribution system used by an insurer does not appear to affect the overall demand for insurance. However, there is a significant negative relationship between the direct writers and the demand for catastrophe coverage. Thus, it appears that use of independent agents is associated with higher sales of catastrophe insurance, all other things held constant.

---

[18] The greater the value of the land, the greater the incentive of an owner to avoid foreclosure if his home is destroyed. This is one reason given for why lenders do not require earthquake insurance in areas of California where land prices are high.

Insurer ownership appears to have a significant effect on demand for insurance in New York. All else being equal, consumers seem to prefer to purchase insurance in general and catastrophe insurance in particular from stockholder-owned insurers, although our regression results indicate consumers have a preference for purchasing non-catastrophe coverage from mutuals.

Further, the ability to purchase home and other insurance coverages from the same company appears to positively influence demand in a manner largely consistent with what we found in Florida.

Also largely consistent with our findings for Florida, firm size does seem to be positively related to the demand for insurance in New York, although the effect is insignificant in the equation for non-catastrophe demand.

In New York, there are only three categories of A.M. Best company ratings in the data set (A+ and higher, A, and A-). The category of A+ and higher is omitted to avoid multicollinearity. For the overall demand equation, there are significant differences among the rating categories and, as was the case with our results for Florida, consumers prefer lower rated companies to the A+ or higher rated category. When we look at the equation for catastrophe demand, we see that A+ or higher is significantly valued over the A companies, but is no different than the A-. One would expect that, if solvency of the company were of paramount concern to the consumer, then we would see both significantly negative coefficients for A and A- companies. This is, in fact, the pattern we see in the non-catastrophic demand equation.

4. GUARANTY FUNDS

To conclude our analysis, we examine the effects of guaranty fund coverage on the demand for insurance. All states have insurance guaranty funds that pay insolvent insurers' claims, but the limits of this coverage vary. In Florida, the limit for fund coverage is $300,000 per claim and, in New York, this limit is $1,000,000.[19] Thus, unpaid losses above those amounts are not covered by the funds, and claimants must attempt to recover these amounts as general creditors against an insurer's estate.[20] This would suggest

---

[19] See http://www.ncigf.org/Publications/Claim%20Parameters.xls for a summary of state fund policy limits for 2001.

[20] Coverages in addition to Coverage A triggered by a given claim would be combined with Coverage A losses in the application of the guaranty fund claim coverage limit. For example, if a fire totally destroyed an insured's home with a Coverage A limit of $250,000 and personal property valued at $125,000, the Florida guaranty fund would only cover $300,000, leaving $75,000 in losses not covered by the guaranty fund.

that consumers with Coverage A limits on their dwellings above these fund limits should pay more attention to their insurers' solvency prospects. We are able to test this hypothesis on the Florida data, as there are ample observations of homes with Coverage A limits above $300,000. For New York, our dataset had too few observations with Coverage A limits over $1,000,000 to test this hypothesis.

Table 5.7 shows our results, focusing on an insurer's A.M. Best rating as the measure of its financial strength. These estimates are derived from models like those shown in Table 5.5, but estimated separately for homes where the Coverage A limit was above or below the Florida fund limit of $300,000 per claim.[21] Panel A shows the results for homes below the $300,000 policy limit for total demand, catastrophe coverage, and non-catastrophe coverage. Once again, the rating level of A+ and above was omitted. Panel A's results for overall demand differ from the results shown in Table 5.5, as that Panel A indicates that consumers prefer A+ companies to A and A- companies. The same is true for non-catastrophe coverage and is consistent with our findings as shown on Table 5.5. For catastrophe coverage, Panel A suggests that consumers prefer A-rated companies to both A+ companies and those rated lower. This suggests that consumers who are fully protected by the funds may be willing to pay more for catastrophe insurance from insurers with good ratings but not the additional premium for insurance from insurers with superior ratings. As explained above, the insurer with the NR2 rating is an anomaly as it is a subsidiary of high-rated insurer.

If a consumer is not fully covered in the event of his insurer's insolvency, then we would expect that he would place a greater value on the insurer's strength. Thus, all coefficients should be negative. This is generally what is observed in Panel B. For the total demand equation, all coefficients are significantly negative (except for the anomalous NR2 company and that is not significantly different from zero).

---

21 We were not able to estimate a fixed effect model here due to the fact that there were some 2000 observations above the $300,000 level. Given the fact that the A.M. Best Ratings do not change much over this period for individual firms, the ratings and the firm effects are highly collinear. If we had a longer panel and we saw ratings change over the time period, we would be able to separate the ratings effect from the firm effect.

Table 5.7

Regression Coefficient Estimates for Various A.M. Best Ratings on the Demand for Insurance (Total, Cat, and Non-Cat) for Policies with Coverage A limits above and below Florida's Guarantee fund Policy Limit ($300K).

Panel A. Effect of Ratings on Households Below Guarantee Fund Policy Limit.

	Rating	Coefficient*	Std. Error	T-stat	Prob
Total Demand	A	-0.2175	0.0252	-8.6300	0.000
	A-	-0.3947	0.0344	-11.4800	0.000
	B+	0.0723	0.0366	1.9800	0.048
	NR2**	0.4643	0.0517	8.9800	0.000
Cat Coverage	A	0.456	0.040	11.440	0.000
	A-	-0.135	0.054	-2.480	0.013
	B+	-0.152	0.058	-2.630	0.009
	NR2	0.379	0.082	4.640	0.000
Non-Cat Coverage	A	-0.222	0.019	-11.620	0.000
	A-	-0.143	0.026	-5.490	0.000
	B+	0.199	0.028	7.160	0.000
	NR2	0.299	0.039	7.610	0.000

Panel B. Effect of Ratings on Households Above Guarantee Fund Policy Limit.

	Rating	Coefficient	Std. Error	T-stat	Prob
Total Demand	A	-0.1247	0.0495	-2.5200	0.012
	A-	-0.4268	0.0686	-6.2200	0.000
	B+	-0.5281	0.2543	-2.0800	0.038
	NR2	0.1192	0.1472	0.8100	0.418
Cat Coverage	A	-0.12107	0.086471	-1.4	0.162
	A-	-0.6943	0.119737	-5.8	0.000
	B+	-1.06289	0.443832	-2.39	0.017
	NR2	0.405322	0.256869	1.58	0.114
Non-Cat Coverage	A	-0.12228	0.026882	-4.55	0.000
	A-	-0.18532	0.037223	-4.98	0.000
	B+	-0.17548	0.137977	-1.27	0.204
	NR2	-0.12237	0.079855	-1.53	0.126

*Regression Coefficients estimates obtained using models like those in Table 4.

**NR2 represents one large company in Florida that is a subsidiary of a well known national company with a current A++ rating. The company was rated NR2 due to its lack of experience. It is currently ranked A by AM Best.

Note that the coefficients are relative to Rating of A+ and Above.

For the overall demand equation, Panel B also shows a logical ordering of the coefficients for the various rating categories reflecting lexiographic preferences (A+ > A> A-> B+). For the catastrophe demand and non-catastrophe demand equations, we see that consumers generally prefer A+-rated companies to other companies, but there are some cases where the coefficients are either insignificant or violate the logical ordering discussed above. Overall, we find evidence that consumers pay greater attention to insurer's financial health when exposed to insolvency risk, as well as evidence of the (not so subtle) moral hazard created by guaranty funds for consumers without this exposure.

This result is similar to that found by Phillips, Cummins, and Allen (1998). While we focus on consumer reaction to perceived solvency risk (as measured by the rating), Cummins, Phillips and Allen focused on how insurers' pricing decisions are influenced by the presence of guaranty funds. Firms with higher default risks had lower prices especially in lines of business (long tail commercial) and are more likely not to be covered by the guaranty fund or that are more likely to have claims above any guaranty fund claim limit.

5. SUMMARY

Our analysis illuminates factors affecting insurance transactions in residential markets subject to different levels of catastrophe risk and regulatory pressure. We estimated the demand for insurance coverage in Florida and New York using two-stage least squares regression and data on insurance contracts, housing and demographic variables, and firm characteristics. We find that the demand for catastrophe coverage is more price elastic than the demand for non-catastrophe coverage. This is true in both Florida and New York. However, the estimated price elasticities for Florida were generally higher in absolute value than the estimated price elasticities for New York, suggesting that price elasticity increases with the cost or price of insurance.

We also found that income elasticities differed between the two states. In Florida, the income elasticity of demand was inelastic, but positive. In New York, we found that the income elasticity was negative for total coverage and for non-catastrophe coverage, implying that these are inferior goods. For catastrophe coverage, the income elasticity in New York was positive and approximately .25, which is close to the Florida result of .32.

We also found that regulatory rate suppression/compression generally increased the demand for insurance in both states but, for New York, the effect was only significant in the equation for catastrophe insurance. Further, the effect of regulatory price constraints was greater in Florida, where a given percentage rate inadequacy (e.g., 10 percent) results in a higher absolute subsidy to the insured. Needless to say, such subsidies in insurance markets come at a high price in terms of their negative effect on incentives for efficient mitigation and location choices.

Some options that expand coverage tended to increase demand, but others tended to lower demand, suggesting that consumers are willing and able to gauge incremental costs against incremental benefits and make the decisions perceived to be in their best interests. Interestingly, higher deductibles were often associated with higher demand. Our explanation is that consumers tend to follow experts' advice to increase their deductibles and use the premium savings to purchase additional coverage that offers a better value in terms of protection against risk.

Finally, we found some evidence that a consumer's exposure to an insurer's insolvency risk (as measured by the amount of a potential total loss that would not be covered by the guaranty fund) affects his valuation of financial strength. Using A.M. Best ratings as a measure of a firm's solvency prospects, we found evidence that consumers with contractual limits below the state guarantee fund policy limit sometimes prefer to purchase coverage from lower rated insurers. In contrast, consumers with contractual limits above the guaranty fund coverage limit appear to consistently prefer buying coverage from higher rated insurers. These results are potentially important for consumer welfare. If state policies with respect to guarantee funds were such that financial strength and other quality indicators were not rewarded in the market place, then the overall quality of the insurance industry providing coverage in a state would suffer and high-risk firms would displace high-quality firms. The consequences for sustainability of the state insurance industry would clearly be deleterious.

Chapter 6

SUMMARY AND CONCLUSIONS

Public attention to the risk of natural disasters and its impact on insurance markets has been partially eclipsed by the terrorism threat, but nature's perils have not subsided. While insurance markets and homeowners have made some essential adjustments in managing catastrophe risk, dislocations remain and a sustainable equilibrium has yet to be reached. Political and regulatory obstacles contribute to a failure to fully come to grips with the hard choices necessary to adequately prepare for the financial fallout of a severe disaster.

This monograph presents the results of the first significant attempt to examine the nature of the demand for insurance against natural catastrophes at a detailed, microeconomic level. We explore several significant aspects of residential insurance markets threatened by hurricanes and constrained by regulation. Importantly, our analysis identifies factors influencing the consumer demand for coverage using a model that properly reflects the interaction of supply and demand. Our work encompasses key variables and their effects on the quantity, quality and price of insurance purchased. We illuminate the sensitivity of demand to prices, household income and other demographic characteristics, policy features and the bundling/unbundling of perils and coverages. Further, we show how regulation has distorted market decisions and thwarted full adjustment to a sustainable market equilibrium in which risk is appropriately priced and sufficient capacity is secured.

A number of observations arise from our analysis. Rates in high-risk coastal areas in Florida have doubled and tripled since Hurricane Andrew, reflecting the reassessment of catastrophe exposure. However, regulation has prevented rates from reaching adequate levels in the highest-risk areas and the pricing gap is growing as other factors (e.g., mold claims) drive up the underlying cost of risk. Although the availability of coverage significantly improved during the latter half of the 1990s, this positive trend reversed in early 2001. As of year-end 2002, state mechanisms provided full or wind coverage for 600,000 homes representing $145 billion in exposures.

A number of homeowners insurers left the Florida market, and others have entered to take their place. Insurers have adjusted the portfolios of properties they cover, but some carriers may retain a high concentration of exposures in southeastern portions of the state to the extent that they have not been transferred back to state mechanisms. Deductibles, particularly for wind, have increased substantially. Insurers and insureds in New York have also experienced the effects of increased catastrophe risk, but to a much lesser degree than in Florida. The differences between the two states reflect the difficulties of political institutions in adjusting to nature's realities.

Within this context of the market structure for homeowners insurance in Florida and New York, we estimated the demand for coverage using two-stage least squares regression and data on insurance contracts, housing and demographic variables, and firm characteristics. Estimated expected loss costs were used to measure the quantity of insurance purchased and the price mark-up or loading to measure price. The quantity of insurance was divided into two components: 1) expected catastrophe losses; and 2) expected non-catastrophe losses. We used this formulation to separately estimate the demands for catastrophe coverage, non-catastrophe coverage, and the total or combined amount of coverage.

Our models estimate the demand effects of standard variables, such as price and income, as well as variables more specific to homeowners insurance transactions subject to catastrophe risk, such as coverage options and an insured's risk characteristics. We find that the demand for catastrophe coverage is more price elastic than the demand for non-catastrophe coverage. However, the Florida price elasticities were higher in absolute value than the New York price elasticities, reflecting among other things the standard result that price elasticity increases with the cost or price of insurance.

We also found that income elasticities (keeping housing values constant) differed between the two states. In Florida, the income elasticity of demand was positive and between .06 and .32. In New York, we found that the income elasticity was negative for total coverage and for non-catastrophe coverage, implying that these are inferior goods. For catastrophe coverage, the income elasticity in New York was positive and .25, which is close to the Florida result. As we noted, these income elasticity results control for housing values. As income increases, however, demand for housing increases as well, with the expected consequence that insurance demand, adjusted for both income and its effects on housing values, will increase. The low income elasticities found in our study do not, of course, contravene this more robust total, positive effect of income on insurance demand in the homeowners market.

We also found that the regulatory rate suppression/compression increased the demand for insurance in both states, although the effect was sometimes insignificant in New York. The effect of regulatory price constraints was greater in Florida, where a given percentage rate inadequacy (e.g., 10 percent) results in a higher absolute subsidy to the insured. While some politicians might view the purchase of more coverage as a positive outcome, the economic implication is diminished homeowner incentives to reduce risk.

When regulators do allow insurers to price coverage options based on their relative costs, consumers can make appropriate choices. Some options that expanded coverage tended to increase demand, while others did not. This suggests that consumers are weighing the incremental benefits against the incremental costs and making the decisions perceived to be in their best interest. Interestingly, higher deductibles were often associated with higher demand. Our explanation is that consumers are rational and tend to follow experts' advice to increase their deductibles and use the premium savings to purchase additional coverage that offers a better value in terms of protection against the risk of more severe losses.

Finally, we found some evidence that a consumer's exposure to an insurer's insolvency risk (as measured by the amount of a potential total loss that would not be covered by the guaranty fund) affects his valuation of financial strength. Using financial strength ratings as a measure of a firm's solvency prospects, we found evidence that consumers with contractual limits below the state guarantee fund policy limit reveal a preference to buy coverage from lower-rated insurers. In contrast, consumers with contractual limits above the guaranty fund coverage limit prefer purchasing coverage from higher-rated insurers. We suspect that insurance agents, considering their exposure to errors and omissions lawsuits, may play a role in steering clients with higher-value properties towards insurers with stronger financial ratings.

In conclusion, insurance markets can play an important role in the effective management of the risk from natural perils. Consumers can respond to accurate price signals to optimize their choices with respect to insurance coverage and risk reduction. Insurers, in turn, can properly manage and diversify their risk exposure and secure their ability to meet their obligations to pay claims in the event that a disaster occurs. Innovations in catastrophe modeling and information management have enables insurers and reinsurers to understand better the risk they face in the catastrophe market and the pricing of these risks in bundled homeowners policies. But a major challenge remains for political institutions and regulatory authorities to allow the effective operation of market forces in allocating resources to the proper financing and mitigation of catastrophe risk.

Appendix A

STRUCTURE-CONDUCT-PERFORMANCE FRAMEWORK

Economists postulate a theoretical relationship between market structure and market results, which is labeled the **structure-conduct-performance hypothesis** (Scherer and Ross, 1990). The basic hypothesis is that market structure determines market conduct, which determines market performance. A market with easy entry and exit and a relatively large number of firms causes firms to behave independently and competitively, which, in turn, leads to good market performance. Exceptions to these conditions and other structural flaws can cause market problems which require regulation, if feasible, to protect consumers and produce market outcomes consistent with the public interest.

Our examination of **market structure** focuses on the number of buyers and sellers and their size distribution, the height of barriers to entry into (and exit from) the market, cost structures, and insurers' geographic concentration. We precede our discussion of market structure with a review of important characteristics of homeowners and dwelling fire/extended coverage insurance policies.

Market conduct refers to the actual behavior (i.e., degree of independence) of firms in setting prices and output levels, product design, advertising, innovation, and capital investment. Our analysis of conduct in catastrophe insurance markets is incorporated into our analysis of their **market performance**, which focuses on price, profit, and output levels, the efficiency of production and allocation, availability, quality of service and solvency.

Analyzing industries like insurance is complicated by the presence of regulation and other forms of government intervention that affect market conditions. This is especially true for catastrophe insurance. Hence, it is important to identify and evaluate government institutions and policies that may significantly influence market behavior, along with other factors. We focus on several aspects of insurance market regulatory policies, as well as government-sponsored insurance facilities. Analyzing government's influence on the market is often a difficult task, given the complex interaction between regulation and market forces, but it is necessary to understanding all of the relevant determinants of market outcomes.

In this monograph, we measure market concentration using concentration ratios at the four-firm (CR4), eight-firm (CR8), and 20-firm (CR20) levels and the Herfindahl-Hirschman Index (HHI). These measures are calculated on a statewide basis for each line and for the U.S. as a whole. A concentration ratio is equal to the combined market share of some number of the top insurers, e.g., CR4 is equal to the combined market share of the top four insurers. These measures reflect the potential market power possessed by the largest firms in a market as well as their risk exposure.[1]

The HHI is equal to the sum of the squared market shares of all firms in the market and can range from near zero to 10,000 (the HHI value when there is only one firm in the market). The higher the HHI, the greater the degree of market concentration. Hence, it measures the degree of concentration throughout the market, not just for some number of the top firms. It also gives more weight to firms with larger market shares, which is consistent with economic theories about the relationship between firms' market shares and the degree of market power they can exercise. According to benchmarks utilized in the U.S. Department of Justice merger guidelines, markets with HHI's less than 2,000 are considered to have a low or moderate degree of concentration and are less likely to be subject to anti-trust restrictions on mergers and acquisitions.[2]

Note that concentration is measured by insurer groups, plus non-affiliated insurers, which better reflects the implications of concentration for competition. Insurers within a group are under common control and typically do not compete with each other. In this monograph, the term "insurers" refers to insurer groups and non-affiliated insurance companies, and the term "insurance companies" refers to individual insurance companies affiliated within groups as well as non-affiliated insurance companies. These tables also are constructed from NAIC data and hence do not include any insurers that do not report to the NAIC.[3] Concentration is measured by insurers' share

---

1 These concentration measures are somewhat crude indicators of catastrophe risk exposure as they are based on statewide data. An insurer's market share could vary significantly among different areas within a state with different degrees of catastrophe risk.

2 The degree of market concentration is only one factor that affects structural competition in a market. Concentration in catastrophe insurance markets is of interest with respect to its impact on competition as well as its implications for catastrophe risk.

3 All multi-state insurers and most larger single-state insurers report data to the NAIC. Some smaller single-state insurers report to the NAIC and others do not. Business written

of premiums written, which will be affected by pricing differences as well as insurers' number of exposures and the amount of insurance coverage provided. Insurers were included in our analysis if they had positive direct premiums written. Companies or groups with zero or negative direct writings, even if possessing a license, were excluded.[4]

through assigned risk plans, FAIR plans and windstorm/beach pools should be reflected in the data reported to the NAIC.

[4] This leaves the discussion of the possibility of potential competition for further study. A license may be a necessary requirement for selling business within a state, but there is also some technical expertise that goes with pricing a given line or effectively servicing a given line. The presence or absence of a license does not necessarily imply anything about these two competencies, nor does it imply anything about the ability of potential new entrants to obtain licenses.

Appendix B

INTRODUCTION TO CATASTROPHE MODELING[1]

As noted in the text at several junctures, catastrophe modeling has become a foundation for ratemaking and exposure management in insuring against the losses of natural catastrophes such as earthquakes, hurricanes, tornadoes, and floods. This Appendix provides a brief introduction to the structure of catastrophe modeling, following the methodology pioneered by AIR Worldwide Corporation (AIR). The interested reader can obtain additional information on the structure and use of such models in Kunreuther et al. (2003).

Fortunately, catastrophes are infrequent. But it is exactly their infrequency that makes the estimation of losses from future catastrophes so difficult. The scarcity of historical loss data makes standard actuarial techniques of loss estimation inappropriate for catastrophe losses. Furthermore, the usefulness of the loss data that does exist is limited because of the constantly changing landscape of insured properties. Property values change, along with the costs of repair and replacement. Building materials and designs change, and new structures may be more or less vulnerable to catastrophe events than were the old ones. New properties continue to be built in areas of high hazard. Therefore, the limited loss information that is available is not suitable for directly estimating future losses. Catastrophe modeling technologies are an alternative to the actuarial and/or "rule of thumb" approaches that had previously been relied upon for the estimation of potential catastrophe losses.

---

[1] This appendix is courtesy of AIR Worldwide Corporation and is reprinted here with permission. As noted in the text, other catastrophe models, both private and public, have also been developed. The reader is referred to the Kunreuther et al. (2003) for further details on the use of catastrophe models in insurance and reinsurance applications.

1. AIR CATASTROPHE MODELING TECHNOLOGY

Fifteen years ago, in 1987, AIR developed a modeling technology based on sophisticated stochastic simulation procedures and computer models of how natural catastrophes behave and act upon the man-made environment. The years since the inception of this new approach have seen the models undergo a continual process of review, refinement, enhancement, and validation. New models continue to be developed for new perils and new regions of the globe.

Figure 1.1 below illustrates the component parts of the AIR catastrophe models. It is important to recognize that each component, or module, represents both the analytical work of the research scientists and engineers who are responsible for its design and the computer programs that run the simulations.

Figure B.1: Catastrophe Model Components (shaded)

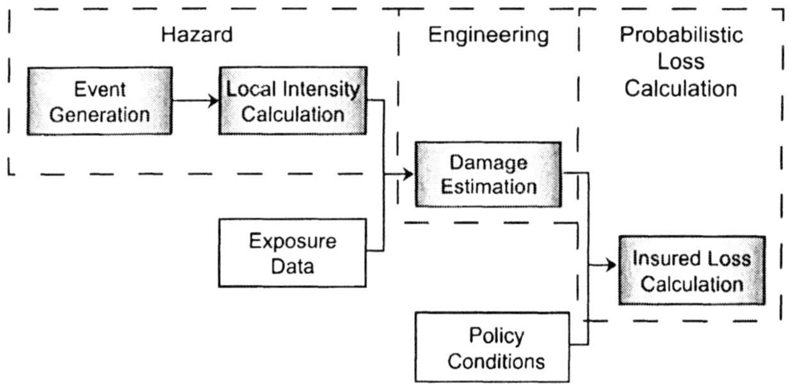

2. EVENT GENERATION MODULE

The event generation module specifies the frequency, magnitude, and other characteristics of potential catastrophe events by geographic location. This requires, among other things, a thorough analysis of the characteristics of historical events.

Catastrophe events are complex and their characterization requires the use of large numbers of variables. A number of leading catastrophe modeling companies collect the available scientific and historical data pertaining to these variables from many different sources. Those companies tabulate and cross-verify all data to the extent possible. When data from different sources conflict, a detailed analysis and the use of expert judgment is required before they are suitable for modeling purposes.

After rigorous data analysis, researchers develop probability distributions for each of the variables, testing them for goodness-of-fit and robustness. The selection and subsequent refinement of these distributions are based not only on the expert application of statistical techniques, but also on well-established scientific principles and an understanding of how catastrophic events behave.

These probability distributions are then used to produce a large catalog of simulated events. By sampling from these distributions, the model generates simulated "years" of event activity. Note that a simulated year represents a hypothetical year of catastrophe experience that could happen in the current year. Typically, catastrophe models allow for the possibility of multiple events occurring within a single year. That is, each simulated year may have no, one, or multiple events, just as might be observed in an actual year. Many thousands of these scenario years are generated to produce a complete and stable range of potential annual experience of catastrophe event activity, and to ensure full coverage of extreme (or "tail") events, as well as full spatial coverage.

3. LOCAL INTENSITY MODULE

Once the model probabilistically generates the characteristics of a simulated event, it propagates the event across the affected area. For each location within the affected area, local intensity is estimated. This requires, among other things, a thorough knowledge of the geological and/or topographical features of a region and an understanding of how these features are likely to influence the behavior of a catastrophe event. The intensity experienced at each site is a function of the magnitude of the event, distance from the source of the event, and a variety of local conditions. Catastrophe model researchers base their calculations of local intensity on empirical observation as well as on theoretical relationships between the variables.

4. DAMAGE MODULE

AIR scientists and engineers have developed mathematical functions called damageability relationships, which describe the interaction between buildings, both their structural and nonstructural components as well as their contents, and the local intensity to which they are exposed. Damageability functions have also been developed for estimating time element losses. These functions relate the mean damage level as well as the variability of damage to the measure of intensity at each location. Because different structural types will experience different degrees of damage, the damageability relationships vary according to construction materials and occupancy. The AIR catastrophe model estimates a complete distribution around the mean level of damage for each local intensity and each structural type, and from there constructs an entire family of probability distributions. Losses are calculated by applying the appropriate damage function to the replacement value of the insured property.

Figure B.2: A Representative Damage Function

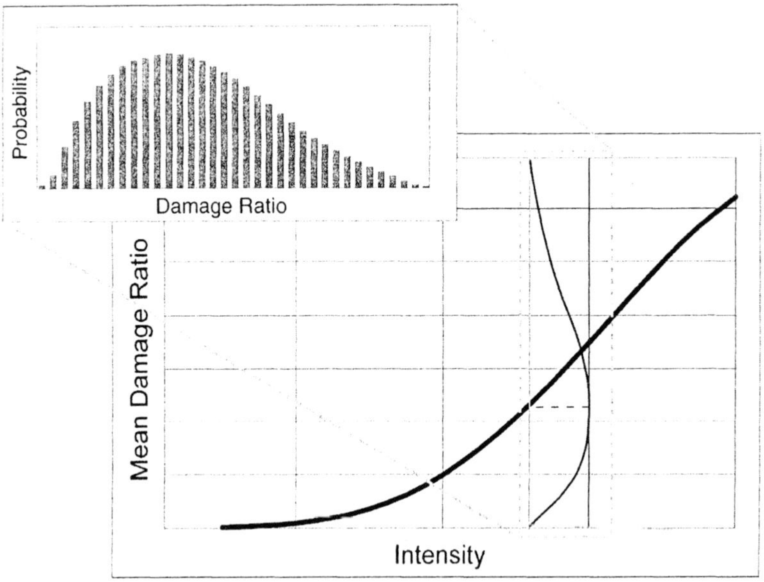

The AIR damageability relationships incorporate the results of engineering studies, tests, and structural calculations. They also reflect the relative effectiveness and enforcement of local building codes. Engineers refine and validate these functions through the use of post-disaster field survey data and through an exhaustive analysis of detailed loss data from actual events supplied to AIR by client companies.

5. INSURED LOSS MODULE

In this last component of the catastrophe model, insured losses are calculated by applying the policy conditions to the total damage estimates. Policy conditions may include deductibles by coverage, site-specific or blanket deductibles, coverage limits and sublimits, loss triggers, coinsurance, attachment points and limits for single or multiple location policies, and risk specific reinsurance terms.

An important feature of the insured loss component of AIR catastrophe models is its handling of multiple location policies. If a policy covers multiple locations under a single policy limit, or with a blanket deductible, etc., the estimated probability distribution of damage at each location (for each event) must first be combined with the distributions from all other locations. This is accomplished through a full convolution process to obtain the precise shape of the resulting distribution, rather than by approximating the combined distribution using a mean and standard deviation.

Figure B.3: Damage Distribution Convolution Logic

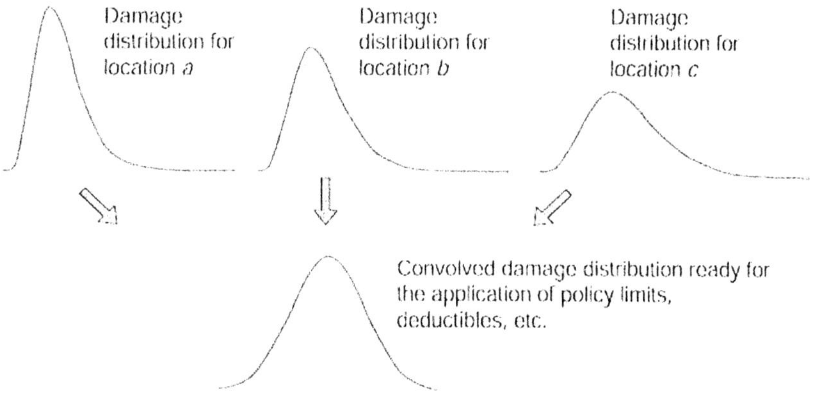

6. MODEL OUTPUT

After all of the insured loss estimations have been completed, they can be analyzed in ways of interest to risk management professionals. For example, the model produces complete probability distributions of losses, also known as exceedance probability curves (see Figure 1.4). Output includes probability distributions of gross and net losses for both annual aggregate and annual occurrence losses. The probabilities can also be expressed as return periods. That is, the loss associated with a return period of 10 years is likely to be exceeded only 10 percent of the time or, on average, in one year out of ten. For example, the model may indicate that, for a given regional book of business, $70 million or more in insured losses would be expected to result once in 50 years on average in a defined geographical area, and that losses of $175 million or more would be expected, on average, once every 250 years.

Output may be customized to any desired degree of geographical resolution down to location level, as well as by line of business, and within line of business, by construction class, coverage, etc. The model also provides summary reports of exposures, comparisons of exposures and losses by geographical area, and detailed information on potential large losses caused by extreme "tail" events.

Figure B.4: Exceedance Probability Curve (Occurrence)

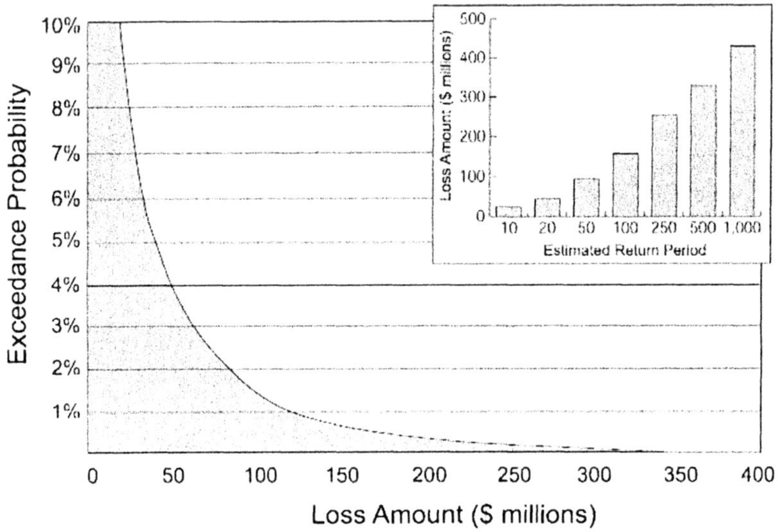

Recent years have witnessed a transfer of catastrophe risk to the capital markets through the issuance of catastrophe, or "cat", bonds. A cat bond is a security with payouts to investors and issuers that depend on "triggers" related to the magnitude and possibly location of catastrophe events. For example, the simplest such cat bond might pay bond holders a 10% return if no significant seismological event occurs in a given year in a given State, 5% if at least one event occurs having a Richter Scale magnitude between 6.0 and 7.0 and –50% (i.e., a loss of half the principle of the bondholders) if at least one event occurs with a Richter Scale magnitude in excess of 7.0. Clearly, investors would be keen to know, before investing, what the probabilities of these various event scenarios are. Catastrophe models provide both the basic answer and the ability to do sensitivity analysis on the robustness of the answer.

REFERENCES

A.M. Best Company. 2001. *Best's Aggregates and Average: Property/Casualty*, Oldwick, NJ.

Applied Insurance Research, Inc. (AIR). 2001. "Probable Maximum Loss Estimates," unpublished tables and figures. Cambridge, MA.

Arrow, Kenneth J. 1971. *Essays in the Theory of Risk Bearing*. Chicago: Markham Publishing Co.

Babbel, David F. 1985. "The Price Elasticity of Demand for Whole Life Insurance," *Journal of Finance* 40 (no. 2, March): 225-239.

Bantwell, Vivek J. and Howard Kunreuther. 2000. "A Cat Bond Premium Puzzle?" *Journal of Psychology and Financial Markets* 1(1): 76-91.

Bartlett, Dwight K., Robert W. Klein, and David T. Russell. 1999. "Attempts to Socialize Insurance Costs in Voluntary Insurance Markets: The Historical Record," *Journal of Insurance Regulation* 17: 478-511.

Berger, Allen N., J. David Cummins, and Mary A. Weiss. 1997. "The Coexistence of Multiple Distribution Systems for Financial Services: The Case of Property-Liability Insurance," *Journal of Business* 70: 515-546.

Barnett, B.J. and J.R. Skees. 1996. "Region and Crop Specific Models of Demand for Federal Crop Insurance," *Journal of Insurance Issues* 19:47-65.

Brown. Mark and Robert E. Hoyt. 1999. "The Demand for Flood Insurance: Empirical Evidence," Working Paper at SSRN.com http://papers.ssrn.com/paper.taf?ABSTRACT_ID=169448.

Briys, Eric, Georges Dionne, and Louis Eeckhoudt. 1989. "More on Insurance as a Giffen Good," *Journal of Risk and Uncertainty* 2: 415-420.

Cao, T., M. Petersen, C. Cramer, T. Toppozada, M. Reichle, and J. Davis. 1999. "The calculation of expected loss using probabilistic seismic hazard," *Bull. Seism. Soc. Amer.* 89: 867-876.

Cleeton, David, and Bruce Zellner. 1993. "Income, Risk Aversion, and the Demand for Insurance," *Southern Economic Journal* 60: 146-56.

Cohen, Marc and Maurice Weintrobe. 2000. *Tax Deductibility of Long Term Care Insurance Premiums*, Mimeo, Health Insurance Association of America, http://membership.hiaa.org/pdfs/000308LTC.pdf.

Collins Center for Public Policy. 1995. *Final Report of the Academic Task Force on Hurricane Catastrophe Insurance*, Tallahassee, FL.

Conning Insurance Research & Publication. 1998. *State Market Analysis for Property-Casualty Insurance 1997*, Hartford, CT: Conning & Company.

Cummins, J. David. 1988. "Risk Based Premiums for Insurance Guaranty Funds," *Journal of Finance* 43: 823-839.

Cummins, J. David. 1990. "Multi-Period Discounted Cash Flow Ratemaking Models in Property-Liability Insurance," *Journal of Risk and Insurance* 57: 79-109.

Cummins, J. David, David Lalonde, and Richard D. Phillips. 2002. "Managing Risk Using Index-Linked Catastrophic Loss Securities," in *Alternative Risk Strategies* edited by Morton Lane. London: Risk Books.

Cummins, J. David, David Lalonde, and Richard D. Phillips. 2003. "The Basis Risk of Index-Linked Catastrophic Loss Securities," *Journal of Financial Economics* forthcoming.

Cummins, J. David, Neil A. Doherty and Anita Lo. 2002. "Can Insurers Pay for the 'Big One'? Measuring the Capacity of an Insurance Market to Respond to Catastrophic Losses," *Journal of Banking and Finance* 26(2): 557-583.

Cummins, J. David, Richard D. Phillips, and Franklin Allen. 1998. "Financial Pricing of Insurance in the Multiple-Line Insurance Company," *Journal of Risk and Insurance* 65: 597-636.

Cummins, J. David, Mary Weiss, and Hong Min Zi. 1999. "Organizational Form and Efficiency: The Coexistence of Stock and Mutual Property-Liability Insurers," *Management Science* 45: 1254-1269.

Davidson, Ross J., Jr. 1996. "Tax-Deductible, Pre-Event Catastrophe Reserves," *Journal of Insurance Regulation* 15: 175-190.

Dionne, Georges and Scott Harrington. ed. 1992. *Foundations of Insurance Economics*, Boston MA: Kluwer Academic Publishers.

FEMA. 2001. *Understanding Your Risks: Identifying Hazards and Estimating Losses*. FEMA Publication 386-2. Washington, DC: FEMA.

Froot, Kenneth A. and Paul G. J. O'Connell. 1999. "On the Pricing of Intermediate Risks: Theory and Application to Catastrophe Reinsurance," in *The Financing of Catastrophe Risks*, edited by Kenneth Froot. Chicago: University of Chicago Press.

Gal-or, E. 1983. "Quality and Quantity Competition," *Bell Journal of Economics* 14: 590-600.

Grace, Martin F., Robert W. Klein, and Paul R. Kleindorfer. 1998. "An Overview of Catastrophe Markets in the U.S.," Working Paper, Wharton Managing Catastrophe Risks Project, University of Pennsylvania.

Grace, Martin F., Robert W. Klein, and Paul R. Kleindorfer. 1999. "The Supply of Catastrophe Insurance under Regulatory Constraints," Working Paper, Wharton Managing Catastrophe Risks Project, University of Pennsylvania.

Grace, Martin F., Robert W. Klein, and Paul R. Kleindorfer. 2000. "The Supply and Demand for Residential Property Insurance with Bundled Catastrophe Perils," Working Paper, Wharton Managing Catastrophe Risks Project, University of Pennsylvania.

Grace, Martin, Robert W. Klein, and Richard D. Phillips. 2001. "An Economic Appraisal of Securitizing Insurance Risk via Onshore Special Purpose Vehicles," *Risk Management and Insurance Review* 4: 7-33.

Green, William. 2000. *Econometric Analysis*, Upper Saddle River, NJ: Prentice Hall.

Greenwald, Bruce C. and Joseph E.Stiglitz. 1990. "Asymmetric Information and the New Theory of the Firm: Financial Constraints and Risk Behavior," *American Economic Review* 80: 106-165.

Harrington, Scott E. and Greg Niehaus. 2001. "Government Insurance, Tax Policy, and the Affordability and Availability of Catastrophe Insurance," *Journal of Insurance Regulation* 19: 591-612.

Herring, Richard J. and Prashant Vankudre. 1987. "Growth Opportunities and Risk-Taking by Financial Intermediaries," *The Journal of Finance* 52: 583-599.

Insurance Information Institute. 2001. *The Fact Book 2001: Property/Casualty Insurance Facts*, New York, N.Y.

Insurance Services Office. 1994a. *The Impact of Catastrophes on Property Insurance*, New York, N.Y.

Insurance Services Office. 1994b. *Catastrophes: Insurance Issues Surrounding the Northridge Earthquake and Other Natural Disasters*, New York, N.Y.

Insurance Services Office. 1996a. *Managing Catastrophe Risk*, New York, N.Y.

Insurance Services Office. 1996b. *Homeowners Insurance: Threats from Without, Weakness Within*, New York, N.Y.

Joskow, Paul L. 1973. "Cartels, Competition and Regulation in the Property-Liability Insurance Industry," *Bell Journal of Economics* 4: 375-427.

Klein, Robert W. 1998. "Regulation and Catastrophe Insurance," in *Paying the Price: The Status and Role of Insurance Against Natural Disasters in the United States*, edited by Howard Kunreuther and Richard Roth, Sr., Washington, D.C.: Joseph Henry Press.

Klein, Robert W. 2000. "Regulating Insurer Solvency in a Brave New World," unpublished working paper, Georgia State University.

Kleindorfer, Paul R. and Robert W. Klein. 2003. "Regulation and Markets for Catastrophe Insurance," in *Advances in Economic Design*, edited by Murat R. Sertel and Semih Koray. Springer Verlag, Heidelberg.

Kleindorfer, Paul R. and Howard Kunreuther. 1999. "Challenges Facing the Insurance Industry in Managing Catastrophe Risks," in *The Financing of Catastrophe Risks*, edited by Kenneth Froot. Chicago: University of Chicago Press.

Kleindorfer, Paul R. and Murat R. Sertel. eds. 2001. *Mitigation and Financing of Catastrophe Risks: Turkish and International Perspectives*, Doordrecht: Kluwer Academic Publishers.

Kunreuther, Howard, Jacqueline Meszaros, Robin Hogarth, and Mark Spranca. 1995. "Ambiguity and Underwriter Decision Processes," *Journal of Economic Behavior and Organization* 26: 337-352.

Kunreuther, Howard. 1996. "Mitigating Disaster Losses through Insurance," *Journal of Risk and Uncertainty* 12: 171-187.

Kunreuther, Howard. 1998a. "Insurability Conditions and the Supply of Coverage," in *Paying the Price: The Status and Role of Insurance Against Natural Disasters in the United States*, edited by Howard Kunreuther and Richard Roth, Sr., Washington, D.C.: Joseph Henry Press.

Kunreuther, Howard. 1998b. "The Role of Insurance in Dealing with Catastrophe Risks from Natural Disasters," in *Alternative Approaches to Insurance Regulation*, edited by Robert W. Klein. Kansas City, Mo.: National Association of Insurance Commissioners.

Kunreuther, Howard. 2002. "The Role of Insurance in Managing Extreme Events: Implications for Terrorism Coverage," *Business Economics* April: 5-16.

Kunreuther, Howard, Patricia Grossi and Chandu Patel. eds. 2003. *New Approaches to the Management of Natural Hazards*, Boston, MAP: Kluwer Academic Publishers, forthcoming.

Lecomte, Eugene and Karen Gahagan. 1998. "Hurricane Insurance Protection in Florida," in *Paying the Price: The Status and Role of Insurance Against Natural Disasters in the United States*, edited by Howard Kunreuther and Richard Roth, Sr., Washington, D.C.: Joseph Henry Press.

Mah, C.H. 2000. "Use of catastrophe models in ratemaking." *Texas Department of Insurance Commissioner's Bulletin* B0037-00. http://www.tdi.state.tx.us/commish/b-0037-0.html

Marlett, David C. and Alan Eastman. 1998. "The Estimated Impact of Residual Market Assessments on Florida Property Insurers," *Risk Management and Insurance Review* 2: 37-49.

Marquis, M. Susan and Stephen H. Long. "Worker Demand for Health Insurance in the Non-Group Market," *Journal of Health Economics* 14(1): 47-63.

Meier, Kenneth J. 1988. *The Political Economy of Regulation - The Case of Insurance*, State University of New York Press.

Mossin, Jan. 1968. "Aspects of Rational Insurance Purchasing," *Journal of Political Economy* 76: 553-68.

Muslin, Rade T. 1996. "Property Insurance Market Crisis," Presentation to the Institute for International Research, March 14, 1996, New York, NY.

Muslin, Rade T. 1997. "Issues in the Regulatory Acceptance of Computer Modeling for Property Insurance Ratemaking," *Journal of Insurance Regulation* 15: 342-359.

Myers, Stewart and Richard Cohn. 1987. "Insurance Rate Regulation and the Capital Asset Pricing Model," in *Fair Rate of Return in Property-Liability Insurance*, edited by J. David Cummins and Scott E. Harrington. Boston, MA: Kluwer Academic Publishers.

National Association of Insurance Commissioners. 2001a. *1999 Dwelling Fire, Homeowners Owner-Occupied, and Homeowners Tenant and Condominium/Cooperative Unit Owner's Insurance*, Kansas City, MO.

National Association of Insurance Commissioners. 2001b. *Profitability By Line By State in 2000*, Kansas City, MO.

Peltzman, Sam. 1976. "Toward a More General Theory of Regulation," *Journal of Law and Economics* 19 (August): 211-40.

Rejda, George E. 2001. *Principles of Risk Management and Insurance*, 7th edition, Boston, MA: Addison Wesley Longman.

Risk Management Solutions, Inc. and Insurance Services Office, Inc. 1995. *Catastrophe Risk*, Menlo Park, CA and New York, N.Y.

Rothschild, Michael and Joseph Stiglitz. 1976. "Equilibrium in Competitive Insurance Markets: An Essay on the Economics of Imperfect Information," *Quarterly Journal of Economics* 90: 629-650.

Russell, Thomas and Dwight M. Jaffee. 1997. "Catastrophe Insurance, Capital Markets, and Insurable Risk," *Journal of Risk and Insurance* 64: 205-230.

Scherer, F. M. and Ross, 1990, *Industrial Market Structure and Economic Performance*, 3rd ed. Chicago: Rand McNally.

Sherdan, William A. 1984. "An Analysis of the Determinants of Demand for Automobile Insurance," *The Journal of Risk and Insurance* 51 (no. 1, March): 49–62.

Stone, James. 1973. "A Theory of Capacity and the Insurance of Catastrophe Risks," *Journal of Risk and Insurance* 40:231-243, 337-355.

Vinson, B. and T.H. Miller. 2000. Pilot project: Eugene-Springfield earthquake damage and loss estimate final report, January 1999. *Oregon Dept. of Geol. and Mineral Industries Open-File Rept. O-00-02.*

Willig, Robert D. 1976. "Consumer Surplus without Apology," *American Economic Review* 66: 589-97.

NAME INDEX

SUBJECT INDEX